STAR
O F   T H E
KING

STAR
OF THE
KING

THE CHRISTIAN'S GUIDE TO
LEARNING THE IDENTITY OF THE
STAR OF BETHLEHEM

Jeffrey W. Mardis

Sword-In-Hand Publishing
Campbellsville, KY

Star of the King

The Christian's Guide to
Learning the Identity of the Star of Bethlehem

by Jeffrey W. Mardis

PUBLISHER'S NOTE:
All Scripture quotations taken from the *Authorized King James Version of the Holy Bible*. All-caps added for emphasis and does not represent an alteration of the text. Any other deviations therefrom are not intentional and do not represent an alteration of the text. Cover and back cover illustration and design, and interior design and layout by Jeffrey Mardis. Certain illustrations in this work are used via the Creative Commons Attribution-Share Alike 3.0 Unported License (CC BY-SA 3.0 US) in cooperation with Distant Shores Media and Sweet Publishing. The use of such illustrations in no way implies an endorsement of said organizations, nor that said organizations endorse the work contained herein. Unless stated otherwise, all other images are in the public domain. Some of the works referenced in this material were cited from the internet and were current at the time of publication. Neither the publisher nor the author are responsible for dead web links or any inaccessible references cited online.

ISBN - 10: 0-9819056-2-5
ISBN - 13: 978-0-9819056-2-4

Greg Miller, Moriah Miller and Jen Miller – proofreaders

Published by:
Sword-In-Hand Publishing
5563 Bengal Road
Campbellsville, KY 42718
Web: www.swordinhandpub.com
E-mail: swordinhandpub@gmail.com

Printed in the United States of America

Other books by Jeffrey W. Mardis from
SWORD-IN-HAND PUBLISHING

What Dwells Beyond
The Bible Believer's Handbook to
Understanding Life in the Universe

Aliens, Angels & Outer Space
A Biblical Investigation into Life Beyond Earth

SWORD
IN HAND™
PUBLISHING

"Open thou mine eyes, that I may behold wondrous things out of thy law."

Psalms 119:18

CONTENTS

PREFACE

Through the years many books have been written concerning the Star of Bethlehem, so why write another? The answer to that is simple. Christians are admonished by scripture to *"Prove all things; hold fast that which is good."* (1Thess. 5:21) Proving a subject centers around *the details* of what God's written word says about a subject. In order to discover those details, however, *Bible study* must come into play (2Tim. 2:15). When looking at the book descriptions presented by the majority of authors who have written on this subject, you will find that, in many cases, in-depth Bible study has been replaced by a study of the stars. While these authors may use Matthew 2:1-11 as a *basis* for their books, their "studies" are not studies of the BIBLE, but studies in ASTRONOMY. This deprives the Christian of God's full counsel. Don't get me wrong, I'm all for using science to undergird scripture. But when science is consulted to the exclusion of scripture, then *that's* when we

XII

have a problem. The word of God should always come first. That's what this book is about – putting the *King James Bible* FIRST. First before science, before opinion, before anything else. Doing so will place the Christian on the road to sound doctrine.

Using only the words of God's Book, this book takes the study of Bethlehem's Star farther than simply its immediate context. It goes beyond Matthew 2:1-11, and shows the Christian how many other scriptures shed light on the subject, light otherwise unattainable through the reading of a handful of Bible verses, or by diverting the study to science alone. It is my prayer that this work will glorify the Lord Jesus Christ, and edify those wanting to know more about the mystery behind the Star of Bethlehem.

"To the law and to the testimony: if they speak not according to this word, it is because there is no light in them" Isaiah 8:20

"Holding fast the faithful word as he hath been taught, that he may be able by sound doctrine both to exhort and to convince the gainsayers." Titus 1:9

Even so, come, Lord Jesus (Rev. 22:20)

Jeffrey W. Mardis

GOD OF NATURE 1 ✳

"Thus saith the LORD, which giveth the sun
for a light by day, and the ordinances of the moon
and of the stars for a light by night, which divideth
the sea when the waves thereof roar;
The LORD of hosts is his name"
Jeremiah 31:35

The Star of Bethlehem is one of the most widely known accounts in all of scripture. During the Christmas season billions of people around the world are exposed to the story, and reminded of the event through the imagery of Christmas cards, Christmas programs, nativity scenes, and the star atop the Christmas tree. Many books have been written on the subject. The vast majority of these books, whether written by Christians or others, the internet retail giant Amazon.com, shows that 95% are based around the science of ASTRONOMY. Since the Bible narrative mentions a "star" this is understandable. But it also means that nearly every author has put all their eggs into one basket. Doing so has helped create the perception that the reality of the Star stands or falls solely on the proofs of science. Of these theories, the most popular are based on:

1.) The interactions and near-passings of planets with other planets, primarily Jupiter, Saturn or Venus (astronomy labels these events as planetary "conjunctions").

2.) Stars, star constellations and other celestial phenomena like comets or supernovae.

3.) Outright denial of the Bible and unconventional theories (like UFO's) have also been proposed.

Very few authors, if any, rely on scripture alone.

Today, the most popular study addressing the Star is a Christian documentary published in May, 2009. At the time of this writing, the video had garnered over 591 four-star and five-star reviews from Amazon.com customers (with the DVD's popularity continuing to grow by the week). Titled *The Star of Bethlehem: Unlocking the Mystery of the World's*

IMAGES/Internet

False theories on the Star of Bethlehem

The Bible & Flying Saucers (above, left), by Presbyterian minister Barry H. Downing, has been in circulation (off and on) since 1968. The author proposes that the UFO phenomena is "of God", and "flying saucer" activity, even today, represents God's angels at work. He further states that many miracles of the Bible were the work of such saucers. This includes the parting of the Red Sea, Ezekiel's wheel, Elijah's chariot, and the Star of Bethlehem. *ForteanTimes* (above, right) is a magazine based around the early works of Charles Fort (1874-1932). It's been in publication since 1973, and covers strange and unexplained phenomena from around the world. Note that the cover of the January, 2011 issue theorizes what the wise men "really saw" was a space ship from another planet.

Most Famous Star, this documentary uses computer software to backtrack the movement of the heavens, and concludes that a series of celestial events collectively contributed to the phenomena. This theory centers primarily around the planet JUPITER. The official website for the documentary states:

"JUPITER. The name of the greatest god of Roman mythology. And the name of the largest planet of our solar system. Jupiter has been known from ages-old to the present as the King Planet. ... SINCE HUMANS HAVE ASSIGNED KINGLY QUALITIES TO THIS GIANT wanderer for dozens of centuries, might it have something to do with our Star announcing the birth of a king? THAT WILL BE OUR WORKING THEORY. ... TO BE MATTHEW'S STAR, JUPITER as viewed from Earth would have to do peculiar things." [1]

IMAGE/Internet

The video then proceeds to track the planet as it produces a sequence of four "conjunctions" and two encounters with star constellations. First, a triple encounter with Regulus[2]

---

[1] Larson, Frederick A. "A Coronation." . Frederick A. Larson, 2014. Web. May 2014. <http://www.bethlehemstar.net/starry-dance/coronation/>. Emphasis added.

[2] Ibid.

[3] Larson, Frederick A. "The Birth of a King." . Frederick A. Larson, 2014. Web. May 2014. <http://www.bethlehemstar.net/starry-dance/the-birth-of-a-king/>.

and Leo[3], then with Virgo[4], and finally, the planet Venus[5]. This implies that the celestial journey of Jupiter signified "the star of Bethlehem" by its interaction with one star, two star constellations, and another planet. According to the video, all this agrees with the Bible. Maybe in a very general sense, but there are things left wanting. Because the Jupiter Theory, by far, seems to be the most popular explanation for the Star, it will be mentioned frequently throughout this book. This is not done to necessarily single-out or pick on *this* particular Christian position, many books propose similar theories. But the high praise and popularity of this video, I believe, helps demonstrate that people are looking in the wrong place for answers.

I can certainly see why Christians may view certain astronomical theories as being significant, after all, the *"...heavens declare the glory of God; and the firmament sheweth his handywork."* (Psa. 19:1) That much we can agree upon. But because of scripture, I do not believe that any of these theories represent "the star" which lead the wise men to Bethlehem. The naked eye was all the ancients used to observe the heavens. They had no telescopes. Because of this, star and planetary movement was not immediately recognizable until the charts, measurements

[4] Larson, Frederick A. "The Birth of a King." . Frederick A. Larson, 2014. Web. May 2014. <http://www.bethlehemstar.net/starry-dance/the-birth-of-a-king/>..

[5] Larson, Frederick A. "Westward Leading." . Frederick A. Larson, 2014. Web. May 2014. <http://www.bethlehemstar.net/starry-dance/westward-leading/>.

and calculations of several days were compared. This helps illustrate that such space-based phenomena would have been too small, happened too slow, and been too far away to have the kind of meaningful impact which Matthew's account requires. Did celestial events happen around the time of Christ's birth? Yes, "around that time". Were any of these events "the star" of Bethlehem? I don't think so. And I don't believe the scriptures support that position either. Yes, at the time, there were unique interactions between planets, stars and star constellations, but none were "the star".

Those who rely on nature alone to explain or interpret the Bible are many times tempted to down-play the Bible's details. Yet truth comes by "every word of God" (Prov. 30:5, Matt. 4:4). If theories of natural phenomena are not in accord with "every word of God", regardless of the event in question, then those theories need to be thrown out. When Aaron's rod transformed into a serpent, it did not line up with science (Ex. 7:9-10). When Moses turned the waters to blood, it did not line up with science (Ex. 7:19-20). When Moses parted the Red Sea, it did not line up with science (Ex. 14:21-22). When Christ walked on the water, it did not line up with science (Mk. 6:48-49). So what? If your "reality" extends no further than your five sense (seeing, hearing, smelling, tasting and touching), then you're in for a SHOCK (Rom. 1:20, John 20:24-29, Heb. 11). This book aims to rely on scripture alone for our answers. By putting the details of God's words FIRST, we automatically align with God, and eliminate any theory that doesn't fall in line with what He's already said – regardless if "science" agrees with the conclusion or not.

> *"...yea, LET GOD BE TRUE, but every man a liar; as it is written, That thou mightest be justified in thy sayings, and mightest overcome when thou art judged."* Romans 3:4

God's words are more than sufficient in their ability to reveal truth. And I believe that there are many scriptural indicators which point to the solution of this mystery. By comparing scripture with scripture, this book will present the study on how the Bible-believing Christian can arrive at that answer. To follow this study no knowledge in astronomy is necessary. No knowledge in ancient Hebrew or Greek is necessary. All one needs is a *King James Bible* and a believing heart and mind. If you have *that*, you have all the tools necessary for a profitable and doctrinally-sound outcome (1 Thess. 2:13). This first chapter will launch our study, and begin with how God controls, interacts and regulates NATURE.

Natural or Supernatural

The primary window of time with which our study of the Star of Bethlehem is concerned, is between the time just after the birth of Christ (Luke 2:7), and the time just prior to Joseph, Mary and the Babe being warned to flee into Egypt

(Matt. 2:13). This is about a two-year time span (more on this later). Within this time the miraculous appearance of the Star occurs. A unique event in history which had never happened before or since. But before we delve into the details of the Star, a few other things need to first be ironed out. Things which are critical to understanding what happened on that night of all nights some 2,000-plus years ago.

The question which needs to be answered, before getting to the text directly, is the question of whether the Star of Bethlehem was (1) a natural phenomenon, or (2) a supernatural phenomenon. Did the Lord GUIDE A NATURAL EVENT to coincide with the birth of Christ and to represent the "star" (like a conjunction of planets), or did He USE MORE UNNATURAL MEANS which have nothing to do with astronomical studies (like signs and wonders)? The truth is, HE COULD HAVE DONE EITHER.

First, the Christian must realize that the words "natural event" are a misnomer. This is because scoffers like to say that if the Star of Bethlehem was a "naturally occurring" event, then God was not its source. The use of the word "natural" is usually a buzzword used by skeptics to imply "without God", meaning that "nature accidentally did it" and God didn't. The argument is that ancient peoples were too dumb to understand certain "natural events", and therefore wrongly attributed such phenomena to "God". Undoubtedly such things have happened among pagan peoples, but this has nothing to do with Matthew's record or the Star of Bethlehem. The Lord is the Author of nature (it didn't author itself), and most events in His creation, in one way or another, are a direct result of His actions. So, if the Star of Bethlehem resulted from a "natural" event (as many popular theories suggest), does that mean the Lord was any less involved? No. It simply means His actions can be scientifically verified. The scriptures testify:

"...the LORD HATH HIS WAY in the WHIRLWIND and in the STORM, and the CLOUDS are the dust of his feet." Nahum 1:3

"Fire, and hail; snow, and vapour; stormy wind FULFILLING HIS WORD." Psalm 148:8

All six of the different elements listed above are found in nature (fire, wind, rain, hail, snow, vapor). Admittedly, the scriptures show that God often uses these as a means of "fulfilling His word". From man's perspective, this means that certain instances which outwardly appear to be meaningless ACCIDENTS OR COINCIDENCES OF NATURE, are actually PLANNED EVENTS OF GOD. Let's look at this a little closer.

The Ordinances of Nature

"[35] Thus saith the LORD, which giveth the SUN for a light by day, and the ORDINANCES OF THE MOON AND OF THE STARS for a light by night,

which divideth the sea when the waves thereof roar; The LORD of hosts is his name: [36] If THOSE ORDINANCES depart from before me, saith the LORD, then the seed of Israel also shall cease from being a nation before me for ever." Jer. 31:35-36

Because God is the Creator of nature, He is the Author of its actions. That's elementary. Here the scriptures demonstrate that PART of those actions include regulating the behavior of celestial bodies like the sun, moon and stars. The sun rises and sets in accord with its established ordinance. The moon waxes and wanes in accord with its established ordinance. The stars twinkle and shine in accord with their established ordinances. The seas wave and roar in accord with their established ordinances. For many, these ordinances are seen as occurring "naturally", without God's help, but the Lord does not need to intervene in these situations directly in order for their actions to be in accord with His Will. God's pre-established laws have determined the timing and outcome of nature, without His direct minute-by-minute guidance. This guidance was instituted at the time of their creation. Modern man calls this guiding force the "laws of nature" (or sometimes blasphemously, "Mother Nature"). The Bible calls it "the ordinances" of God. This is how the sun, moon, stars, fire, wind, rain, hail, snow and vapor are constantly "fulfilling his word" no matter what it may appear to be doing "naturally". This applies to all of nature.

IMAGE/Bigstockphoto.com   The ordered movement of the solar system

The Ordinances of God regulate all of nature. Part of these ordinances control the movement of the heavens. Science refers to these ordinances as "the laws of nature", a misnomer which wrongly implies that all such movements are coincidental or accidental.

"Thy faithfulness is unto all generations: thou hast ESTABLISHED THE EARTH, and IT ABIDETH. THEY CONTINUE THIS DAY ACCORDING TO THINE ORDINANCES: for all are thy servants."

Psalm 119:90-91

However, there are also times when the Lord intervenes in these guiding laws.

The Supernatural Manipulation of Nature

Storms are a daily occurrence on planet earth. Weather patterns are a result of the laws and ordinances of God.

"[23] And when he was entered into a ship, his disciples followed him. [24] And, behold, THERE AROSE A GREAT TEMPEST IN THE SEA, insomuch that the ship was covered with the waves: but he was asleep. [25] And his disciples came to him, and awoke him, saying, Lord, save us: we perish. [26] And he saith unto them, Why are ye fearful, O ye of little faith? Then he arose, and REBUKED THE WINDS AND SEA; and there was a great calm. [27] But the men marvelled, saying, What manner of man is this, that even THE WINDS AND THE SEA OBEY HIM!"

Matthew 8:23-27

Here we see a clear example of the Lord *intervening* in the ordinances which regulate severe weather events. Because of this, the outcome was altered. These verses show that the storm was powerful enough to drown everyone on the ship (*"...save us: we perish..."*), but this potential was averted (see also Mk. 4:37-38). Note that this everyday behavior of the wind and sea seemed to have a "natural" ending. But instead, its ending resulted from the Lord's direct influence. The Lord simply SPOKE and nature obeyed. There was a collision between GOD'S VOICE and the ORDINANCES OF

IMAGE/Sweet Publishing, sweetpublishing.com   "Peace, be still."

When Christ spoke and stopped the tempest on the Sea of Galilee, those in the boat with him, were probably the only ones which ever knew that the storm had not stopped on its own. (Matt. 8:23-27)

NATURE – and God won. If you had been standing on the seashore, and not in the boat with the disciples, you would have probably concluded that the storm ceased "naturally" –without God's help–you would have been wrong!

Many other happenings can also have an outward appearance of resulting from nature, but are actually the result of God.

"[12] And the LORD appeared to Solomon by night, and said unto him, I have heard thy prayer, and have

chosen this place to myself for an house of sacrifice.
[13] If I SHUT UP HEAVEN that there be NO RAIN,
or if I COMMAND THE LOCUSTS to devour the land,
or if I SEND PESTILENCE among my people; [14]
If my people, which are called by my name, shall
humble themselves, and pray, and seek my face, and
turn from their wicked ways; then will I hear from
heaven, and will forgive their sin, and will heal their
land." 2 Chronicles 7:12-14

"For thus saith the Lord GOD; How much more
when I SEND MY four sore JUDGEMENTS upon
Jerusalem, the SWORD, and the FAMINE, and the
noisome BEAST, and the PESTILENCE, to cut off
from it man and beast?" Ezekiel 14:21

Here God's words show that drought, war, famine, disease, and animal and insect behavior, can be the means by which God sends judgment. And although these all have an appearance of occurring "naturally", they do not happen by accident nor come to pass without purpose. Even simple things like spring showers are events associated with God's mercy and not His judgement. The scriptures testify that He *"...sendeth rain on the just and on the unjust."* (Matt. 5:45)

The point is, many legitimate "acts of God" outwardly appear as "natural" events. This simply means, that sometimes when God intervenes, He intervenes within the confines of His ordinances. When this is done, such events can be explained "scientifically". Because of this, most scientists conclude that "God is not involved". They're wrong. The truth is, sometimes the Lord ALLOWS HIS ORDINANCES TO CONTROL NATURE, and at other times He may PERSONALLY INTERVENE AND CONTROL NATURE HIMSELF. There's no real way of knowing which is which. But it doesn't matter, both instances are cases of God "fulfilling his word". (Psa. 148:8)

Satan & Nature

Another thing we've not mentioned as yet, is that the Adversary (Satan the Devil) can also control certain natural events. He is *"the prince of the power of the air"* (Eph. 2:2), so to exclude him from our discussion is to leave out part of the equation. In the book of Job, the Lord removes His protective hedge from Job and relinquishes Job into the hand of Satan (Job. 1:12). When this is done, Job's animals, servants and family are immediately destroyed. Job is then smitten with boils. The Devil uses four means to bring about this destruction.

1.) Controlling people (Job 1:15 & 17)
2.) Controlling fire (Job 1:16)
3.) Controlling wind (Job 1:19)
4.) Controlling disease (Job 2:4-7)

While Satan is irrelevant to our study on the Star of Bethlehem, I still felt it important to add this to the discussion. Satan is the king of counterfeit, and it's always important to understand the areas where he can mimic God. The manipulation of certain elements in nature (like wind and fire) is one of those areas.

For example, I believe that Satan being "the prince of the power of the air" (Eph. 2:2) is probably why the tempest arose while Christ and his disciples crossed the Sea of Galilee. Of course, there's always the possibility that God allowed His ordinances to bring the storm so "that the works of God should be made manifest" (John 9:3). But if the Devil *is* responsible, it explains a lot. Consider this – the context of the event shows that Christ and his disciples were on their way to the Gadarenes, the home of "Legion", the most devil-possessed man in all the Bible. During their trip a unique event occurs – NATURE RISES UP AGAINST THE LORD. It's entirely possible that, in an effort to protect a demoniac stronghold, Satan raises a storm to slay Jesus and his disciples, but the plot fails (see Matt. 8:23-34; Mk. 4:35-41 & 5:1-17 and Lk. 8:22-37).

A similar event also happens with the apostle Paul. In this example, we find the only reference in scripture where WEATHER PHENOMENA is given a name – EUROCLYDON (yu-ROK-ly-don, Acts 27:14). Was this another unannounced appearance of the Devil? Was "Euroclydon" a name given to "the prince of the power of the air"? Maybe. Was Satan trying to kill Paul? It's possible. Paul does make mention of Satan's hindrance on one occasion (1Thess. 2:18). Perhaps

IMAGE/Sweet Publishing, sweetpublishing.com   Paul encounters Euroclydon

The scriptures point to the possibility that "Euroclydon" was a tempest, conjured by the Devil, in an effort to kill Paul. (Acts 27:14)

he had this incident partially in mind when making the comment? But whether Satan was responsible for the storm on the Sea of Galilee or not, or whether he was responsible for Euroclydon or not, the Bible doesn't explicitly say. But the Devil *is* "the prince of the power of the air", and after comparing scripture with scripture and having a look at its details, the potential is certainly there. Note this – had these combined events succeeded, they would have eliminated persons most central to Christianity – Jesus, Paul and the disciples. Would the Devil have an interest in doing that? Regardless, Satan DOES have the power to manipulate nature. After the Lord lowers His hedge from Job, He says to the Devil; *"...all that he hath is in THY POWER..."* (Job 1:12) To ignore this fact, is to be "ignorant of his devices", and ultimately, ignorant of scripture (2Cor. 2:11).

Chapter Summary

This chapter constitutes the first step in laying the groundwork for understanding the Star of Bethlehem. We've yet to explore the scriptural details of the Star, that will be covered thoroughly a little later in the book, but thus far, we've laid half our foundation. This first half helps us to understand that events which appear to be "natural", like the appearing of a star, have the possibility of happening as a result of three influences.

1.) God's Ordinances of Nature - Nature moves and behaves in accord with the laws and ordinances established by the Creator. These laws and ordinances constitute their "natural" behavior. These ordinances guide nature continually, and do not require God's minute-by-minute oversight. This means that the Star of Bethlehem may have simply been the outcome of ordinances which the Lord established for planets or stars. Most all modern Christian theories regarding Bethlehem's Star fall into this category.

2.) God Intervening in the Ordinances of Nature - Occasionally the Lord intervenes directly with His established ordinances (like when Christ stopped the tempest on the Sea of Galilee).

3.) Satan Intervening in the Ordinances of Nature - Satan can also influence God's ordinances. Satan is known as "the prince of the power of the air" (Eph. 2:2), and can effect the behavior of wind, fire and other seemingly-natural events.

While points 2 and 3 represent supernatural influences upon nature, ALL THREE can outwardly appear as WORKS OF NATURE. Because of this, ALL THREE are scientifically verifiable. This means that both God and the Devil can influence an event, without that event having any obvious "supernatural" indicators. It also means that the use of science to "disprove" the actions of God (or the Devil) is pointless. This is because there are times when science will conclude that "nature did it", when, in fact, points 2 and 3 above show that that's not always the case. Science can be MISLEADING.

"[19] For it is written, I will destroy the wisdom of the wise, and will bring to nothing the understanding of the prudent. [20] Where is the wise? where is the scribe? where is the disputer of this world? hath not God made foolish the wisdom of this world? [21] For after that in the wisdom of God the world by wisdom

knew not God, it pleased God by the foolishness of
preaching to save them that believe."

1Corinthians 1:19-21

The next chapter will take the second step in laying the groundwork for our study. In that chapter the shoe will be on the other foot. Chapter 2 will look at what happens when God steps OUTSIDE of His established ordinances and goes against their "natural" behavior.

GOD OF WONDER 2

"And the LORD shewed signs and wonders,
great and sore, upon Egypt, upon Pharaoh,
and upon all his household, before our eyes:"
Deuteronomy 6:22

I n the previous chapter we looked at how God uses nature to fulfill his word. Even though the Hand of God may be involved, many times when this is done it does not outwardly appear as a miraculous event, but rather, a natural event. This chapter will continue this study, but show God's other method of action – that of signs, wonders and miracles.

The Voice of God & the First Miracles

The first miracles recorded in scripture take place in the very first book and chapter. Genesis 1 chronicles the creation account. Here it is revealed that the universe came into existence via the most powerful force ever described on paper – THE VOICE OF GOD. Genesis 1 describes six instances where the words *"and God said"* created the known universe. This included the speaking-into-existence of light, the firmament (outer space), grass, trees and fruit, the sun, moon and stars, the animals and man. Nearly the entire chapter of Psalm 29 gives glory to the magnificence of this Voice.

[1] Give unto the LORD, O ye mighty, give unto the LORD glory and strength. [2] Give unto the LORD the glory due unto his name; worship the LORD in the beauty of holiness. [3] THE VOICE of the LORD is upon the waters: the God of glory thundereth: the LORD is upon many waters. [4] THE VOICE of the LORD is powerful; the voice of the LORD is full of majesty. [5] THE VOICE of the LORD breaketh the cedars; yea, the LORD breaketh the cedars of Lebanon. [6] He maketh them also to skip like a calf; Lebanon and Sirion like a young unicorn. [7] THE VOICE of the LORD divideth the flames of fire. [8]THE VOICE of the LORD shaketh the wilderness; the LORD shaketh the wilderness of Kadesh. [9] THE

VOICE of the LORD maketh the hinds to calve, and discovereth the forests: and in his temple doth every one speak of his glory. [10] The LORD sitteth upon the flood; yea, the LORD sitteth King for ever. [11] The LORD will give strength unto his people; the LORD will bless his people with peace."

Psalm 29:1-11

And yet while the works in Genesis constitute some of the most jaw-dropping and blatant examples of God's raw power (a power originating from the WORDS of His mouth), these events ARE NOT SIGNS AND WONDERS. Specifically, signs, tokens and wonders are miraculous events used by the Lord TO COMMUNICATE TO MAN (more on this later). During the Genesis creation, man was nowhere around until the very last day, and by that time, had missed the entire event. In Genesis 2:19 we do find an event where the Lord is dealing with Adam, but this is a unique, one-time scenario.

"And out of the ground the LORD God formed every beast of the field, and every fowl of the air; and brought them unto Adam to see what he would call them: and whatsoever Adam called every living creature, that was the name thereof." Genesis 2:19

According to this text, it's very possible that Adam actually *saw* the creation of these animals. But that proposal is debatable. The context seems to indicate that these creatures were created out of Adam's direct line of sight, and then later brought to him for naming. Remember, this event was unique. It was before the creation of woman, and at that time, Adam was the sole human being on planet earth. The Lord did not later CONTINUE TO WORK MIRACLES in the presence or sight of Adam, nor any of his immediate descendants – especially Adam's pre-flood descendants (don't forget that). True signs and wonders do not show up until approximately 2,460 years later. When this happens, the scriptures actually use the words "signs", "tokens", "wonders" or "miracles" in connection with them – words never associated with the miraculous acts of Genesis 1 and 2. While it's true that the first appearance of the word "signs" is connected with the STARS, this type of sign is primarily connected with *the divisions and measurements of time,* not necessarily in connection with the *miracles* of God.

"And God said, Let there be lights in the firmament of the heaven TO DIVIDE THE DAY FROM THE NIGHT; and LET THEM BE FOR SIGNS, and for SEASONS, and for DAYS, and YEARS" Genesis 1:14

However, the second appearance of the word (sign or signs - Ex. 4:8-9) has nothing to do with the sun, moon or stars, nor the divisions of day, night, seasons, days or years. Exodus defines these types of "signs" as God's "wonders", the book of Numbers calls them "miracles", and both are connected with GOD'S DEALINGS WITH ISRAEL.

"And I will stretch out my hand, and smite Egypt with all my WONDERS which I will do in the midst thereof: and after that he will let you go." Ex. 3:20

"[22] Because all those men which have seen my glory, and my MIRACLES, which I did in Egypt and in the wilderness, and have tempted me now these ten times, and have not hearkened to MY VOICE; [23] Surely they shall not see the land which I sware unto their fathers, neither shall any of them that provoked me see it:" Numbers 14:22-23

A Brief History of Signs & Wonders

According to scripture, signs and wonders are events MEANT TO BE SEEN by man that CANNOT BE EXPLAINED by science. For the most part, they are events outside of God's established ordinances. This means that signs and wonders do not conform with the laws of nature. They are beyond nature. They are super-natural. The book of Exodus tells of the first sign and wonder.

"[2] And the angel of the LORD appeared unto him in A FLAME OF FIRE OUT OF THE MIDST OF A BUSH: and he looked, and, behold, THE BUSHED BURNED WITH FIRE, and THE BUSH WAS NOT CONSUMED. [3] And Moses said, I will now turn

Mosses at the burning bush

The burning bush is the first real sign and wonder found in scripture. By this time, the twelve sons of Abraham had grown into a nation, and this miracle marks the beginning of God's dealings with Israel as a whole. The first time in history where the Lord began to work one-on-one with a nation.

aside, and see this GREAT SIGHT, why THE BUSH IS NOT BURNT." Exodus 3:2-3

The significant thing about the burning bush, is that it marks the time when Israel had finally grown into a NATION. A nation birthed while in bondage to Egypt 430 years (Ex. 12:40-41). Before that time Israel was not a nation. It only existed in the persons of Abraham, Isaac and Jacob, and their immediate sons. Here, however, is the first event dealing with Israel as a *nation*. And in this event, we see the

Lord using SUPERNATURAL SIGNS to let Moses know that
He is the Lord God of his fathers.

> *"[4] And when the LORD saw that he turned aside to
> see, God called unto him out of the midst of the bush,
> and said, Moses, Moses. And he said, Here am I. [5]
> And he said, Draw not nigh hither: put off thy shoes
> from off thy feet, for the place whereon thou standest
> is holy ground. [6] Moreover he said, I AM THE GOD
> OF THY FATHERS, the God of Abraham, the God of
> Isaac, and the God of Jacob. And Moses hid his face;
> for he was afraid to look upon God."* Exodus 3:4-6

All the signs, tokens and wonders which Moses (and
Aaron) then proceeded to work upon Egypt (turning a
rod into a serpent; turning water into blood; calling forth
plagues of frogs, flies and lice; calling down hailstones of
fire; plagues of darkness and death, etc.), were all used for
one primary purpose.

> *"THAT THEY MAY BELIEVE that the LORD God of
> their fathers, the God of Abraham, the God of Isaac,
> and the God of Jacob, hath appeared unto thee."*
> Exodus 4:5

Before the burning bush, God had never approached unto
any nation and said; *"Look, I am the Lord God, the Creator
of heaven and earth, and here are my signs and wonders*

that you may believe in me." That had never happened. The burning bush was a NEW and UNIQUE event in history, and signs and wonders were specifically designed for THE EYES OF GOD'S CHOSEN PEOPLE. Remember that Voice we mentioned back in Genesis 1? The SAME VOICE WHICH CREATED THE UNIVERSE with its words, and once walked with Adam "in the garden in the cool of the day" (Gen. 3:8)? Well, at the burning bush, that Voice shows up again.

> *"[33] Did ever people hear THE VOICE OF GOD speaking out of the midst of the fire, as thou hast heard, and live? [34] Or hath God assayed to go and take him a nation from the midst of another nation, by temptations, by SIGNS, and by WONDERS, and by war, and by a mighty hand, and by a stretched out arm, and by great terrors, according to all that the LORD your God DID FOR YOU in Egypt BEFORE YOUR EYES? [35] Unto thee it was SHEWED, THAT THOU MIGHTEST KNOW that the LORD he is God; there is none else beside him."* Deut. 4:33-35

Note the clear rhetorical questions in the verses above. These questions are not asked to elicit information, but to make a statement.

1. - QUESTION: Did ever people hear the voice of God speaking out of the midst of the fire, as thou hast heard, and live? **ANSWER:** No.

IMAGE/Sweet Publishing, sweetpublishing.com   Turning water into blood

The miracles worked upon Egypt by Moses and Aaron, were done so that
Israel would believe and recognize the God of Abraham.

2. - QUESTION: Hath God assayed to go and take
him a nation from the midst of another nation, by
temptations, by signs, and by wonders, and by war, and
by a mighty hand, and by a stretched out arm, and by
great terrors, according to all that the LORD your God
did for you in Egypt before your eyes? **ANSWER:** No.

These texts make three points very clear.

(1) Other than Israel, God has never spoken to a people
as a whole.

(2) Other than Israel, God has never taken a nation unto himself.

(3) Other than Israel, God has never used signs and wonders when dealing with a nation.

Signs and wonders are meant for the eyes of Israel. Other scriptures also reinforce this concept. Note how the Bible communicates that signs and wonders are meant to be seen by the eyes of the people of Israel.

"The LORD your God which goeth before you, he shall fight for you, according to all that he did for you in Egypt BEFORE YOUR EYES;" Deuteronomy 1:30

"But YOUR EYES HAVE SEEN all the great acts of the LORD which he did." Deuteronomy 11:7

"[2] And Moses called unto all ISRAEL, and said unto them, YE HAVE SEEN all that the LORD did BEFORE YOUR EYES in the land of Egypt unto Pharaoh, and unto all his servants, and unto all his land; [3] The great temptations which THINE EYES HAVE SEEN, the SIGNS, and those great MIRACLES" Deut. 29:2-3

"[5] I sent Moses also and Aaron, and I plagued Egypt, according to that which I did among them: and afterward I brought you out. [6] And I brought your fathers out of Egypt: and ye came unto the sea;

IMAGE/Sweet Publishing, sweetpublishing.com   The parting of the Red Sea

Once Israel departed Egypt, the Lord continued to work signs and wonders in their sight.

and the Egyptians pursued after your fathers with chariots and horsemen unto the Red sea. [7] And when they cried unto the LORD, he put darkness between you and the Egyptians, and brought the sea upon them, and covered them; and YOUR EYES HAVE SEEN WHAT I HAVE DONE in Egypt: and ye dwelt in the wilderness a long season." Joshua 24:5-7

"[10] They kept not the covenant of God, and refused to walk in his law; [11] And forgat his works, and his WONDERS THAT HE HAD SHEWED THEM. [12]

Marvellous things did he IN THE SIGHT OF THEIR
FATHERS, in the land of Egypt, in the field of Zoan."
Psalm 78:10-12

When the Lord Jesus was on earth, he was sent "unto the lost sheep of the house of Israel" (Matt. 15:24). And because He knew "the Jews require a sign" (1Cor. 1:22), he worked signs, wonders and miracles during this ministry.

"This BEGINNING OF MIRACLES did Jesus in Cana of Galilee, and manifested forth his glory; and HIS DISCIPLES BELIEVED on him." John 2:11

"Now when he was in Jerusalem at the passover, in the feast day, MANY BELIEVED in his name, WHEN THEY SAW THE MIRACLES which he did." John 2:23

"And a great multitude followed him, BECAUSE THEY SAW HIS MIRACLES which he did on them that were diseased." John 6:2

"Ye MEN OF ISRAEL, hear these words; Jesus of Nazareth, a man APPROVED OF GOD AMONG YOU BY MIRACLES AND WONDERS AND SIGNS, which God did by him IN THE MIDST OF YOU, as ye yourselves also know:" Acts 2:22

Of course, there are no men working signs and wonders today. If there are, they're counterfeit works of the Devil. This

IMAGE/Sweet Publishing, sweetpublishing.com   Christ's first miracle

The Lord Jesus Christ worked signs and wonders so that the Jews would recognize Him as their promised Messiah. His first miracle was turning water into wine – a type and picture of one of Moses' first miracles of turning water into blood.

is because the Lord is currently turned away from Israel "until the fullness of the Gentiles be come in." This is the Church Age, and God does not deal with the Church through signs and wonders. The born-again Christian walks by FAITH, not by SIGHT (2Cor. 5:7). But with Israel it is not so. They walk by faith AND sight, "For the Jews require a sign..." (1Cor. 1:22). For this reason, few Jews will be saved during the age of the Church. But be that as it may, God "hath not cast away his people" (Rom. 11:2).

"Then Paul and Barnabas waxed bold, and said, It was NECESSARY that the word of God should FIRST have been spoken TO YOU [Israel]: but seeing ye put it from you, and judge yourselves unworthy of everlasting life, lo, WE TURN TO THE GENTILES. For SO HATH THE LORD COMMANDED US, saying, I have set thee to be a light of the Gentiles, that thou shouldest be for salvation unto the ends of the earth."
Acts 13:46-47

"For I would not, brethren, that ye should be ignorant of this MYSTERY, lest ye should be wise in your own conceits; that BLINDNESS IN PART [not total blindness] is happened to ISRAEL, UNTIL the fulness of the Gentiles be come in." Romans 11:25

During the coming Great Tribulation (after the Church age has ended, and the Bride of Christ is taken out), SIGNS AND WONDERS WILL REAPPEAR. This is because "the fullness of the Gentiles" will have passed, and God will once again turn back to His people and seal 144,000 "of all the tribes of the children of Israel". This is to preserve part of them through the time of "Jacob's trouble" (see Rev. 7:3-8, Jer. 30:7), a time when a counterfeit Christ will rise and show counterfeit miracles to deceive, not only the unmarked of Israel, but the whole world. Miracles done IN THE SIGHT OF MAN.

"And he [the Antichrist] *doeth GREAT WONDERS, so that he maketh fire come down from heaven on the earth IN THE SIGHT OF MEN, AND DECEIVETH THEM that dwell on the earth BY MEANS OF THOSE MIRACLES which he had power to do..."*

Revelation 13:13-14

Because God will have turned back to Israel, the Great Tribulation is also the time when two witnesses reappear and have the power to turn water into blood, call-forth plagues, stop the rain, and call-down fire from heaven (Rev. 11:5-6). And the two witnesses are men with whom Israel is very familiar. Two men who have *worked wonders in the past*. Men which represent the Law (Moses) and the Prophets (Elijah). Enoch is not one of these witnesses (Gen. 5:18-24). Enoch is not a Jew, Israel never had any dealings with Enoch, and Enoch never worked a single sign or wonder a day in his life. It's absurd to believe that Enoch would play a role during the time of "Jacob's Trouble". Regardless, the main point to get a hold of here, is the purpose behind signs and wonders. These are special miracles of God, outside of nature's laws, which first appeared at the BIRTH OF ISRAEL.

Beyond the Reaches of Science

We can now stand on solid ground and say with authority that, according to scripture, signs and wonders are for the nation of Israel. Most all of these miracles involve some aspect of nature (a bush, water, serpents, locusts, flies, lice, darkness, fire, hail, etc.). But even though they all may have a connection with nature, they also cannot be explained by science. This is because *they take place apart from the ordinances which regulate their behavior.* No amount of studying by "science" can explain something which supersedes the laws of its "natural" actions. For example:

> *"Behold, I will bring again the shadow of the degrees, which is gone down in the sun dial of Ahaz, ten degrees backward. So the sun returned ten degrees, by which degrees it was gone down."* Isaiah 38:8

In this instance we see the SUN MOVING BACKWARD ten degrees. This reverse shift in light caused the shadow of the sundial to also move backward. According to the ordinances which the Lord has established to regulate the movement of the sun, THIS EVENT WAS IMPOSSIBLE. It is something the sun would have NEVER DONE by its ordinances alone. Yet it happened. How? God stepped OUTSIDE of His own "laws of nature" to perform the miracle. It was a visible SIGN to Hezekiah the King of Judah.

"And THIS SHALL BE A SIGN unto thee from the LORD, that the LORD will do this thing that he hath spoken; Behold, I will bring again the shadow of the degrees, which is gone down in the sun dial of Ahaz, ten degrees backward."

Isaiah 38:7-8

IMAGE/Sweet Publishing, sweetpublishing.com   The sundial of Ahaz

All the laws of nature were subverted when the shadow of Ahaz's sundial moved backwards ten degrees. This helps demonstrate that God's miracles are not bound by nature or science. (Isa. 38:7-8)

Supernatural signs, wonders and miracles are beyond the reaches of science. Tough apples.

Chapter Summary

Having discovered in the previous chapter that the Lord has decreed "ordinances" to regulate the behavior of nature, and now having examined when and why God uses signs and wonders, the question which needs answering is this:

When the Star of Bethlehem appeared, was it God using and guiding a natural event, or did God step outside of His nature-guiding ordiances?

Since the Lord can do either, how can we discover which method God used? Easy. God's word plainly states the conditions under which the Star of Bethlehem appeared. It appeared at the time of Christ's birth. A time when God was DEALING WITH ISRAEL. The birth of Christ was the fulfillment of scripture, and the fulfillment of a SIGN AND WONDER, a fact that should not be taken lightly when considering the Star of Bethlehem.

"Therefore the Lord himself shall GIVE YOU A SIGN; Behold, a virgin shall conceive, and bear a son, and shall call his name Immanuel." Isaiah 7:14

In contrast, the reader is reminded that the popular Jupiter Theory is admittedly based, not on scripture, but on the reasoning that "...humans have assigned kingly qualities to this [planet] ...for dozens of centuries..."[6] The Jupiter Theory is centered around a centuries-old idea of "humans" – not an idea of God, Christians or the Bible. This shows the foundational reasons why choosing between the God-using-Jupiter-as-the-Star theory, and God-using-signs-and-wonders-as-the-Star theory, are important. Because Christ's birth was A SIGN TO ISRAEL, supernatural phenomena surrounded the event. Phenomena outside the ordinances which guide nature. Unscientific phenomena like a virgin giving birth, or an appearance of angels – things impossible

---

[6] Larson, Frederick A. "A Coronation." . Frederick A. Larson, 2014. Web. May 2014. <http://www.bethlehemstar.net/starry-dance/coronation/>. Emphasis added.

to explain-away "naturally". Because of these guiding circumstances and their undergirding scriptures, I believe the Star of Bethlehem was not simply a guided natural event (like Jupiter or a conjunction of stars and planets). It was something MORE. In the chapters that follow we will examine in detail what this "MORE" entails.

"Thou art the God that doest wonders: thou hast declared thy strength among the people." Psalms 77:14

STAR OF WONDER 3

"...and, lo, the star, which they saw in the east, went before them, till it came and stood over where the young child was."

Matthew 2:9

This chapter will cover two accounts dealing with the birth of Christ and the interval in which the Star of Bethlehem appears. As stated previously, the primary window of time with which our study is concerned is about a two-year time frame. This period falls between the time just after the birth of the Lord Jesus (Luke 2:7), and just prior to Joseph, Mary and Babe escaping into Egypt (Matt.

2:13). The purpose of this chapter is to get the full account of circumstances surrounding the Star. This context, in conjunction with chapters 1 and 2, will then be used to build our answers.

The Star Appears

The book of Matthew contains the Bible's only account of the Star of Bethlehem.

[1] Now when Jesus was born in Bethlehem of Judaea in the days of Herod the king, behold, there came wise men from the east to Jerusalem,

[2] Saying, Where is he that is born King of the Jews? for we have seen his star in the east, and are come to worship him.

[3] When Herod the king had heard these things, he was troubled, and all Jerusalem with him.

[4] And when he had gathered all the chief priests and scribes of the people together, he demanded of them where Christ should be born.

[5] And they said unto him, In Bethlehem of Judaea: for thus it is written by the prophet,

[6] And thou Bethlehem, in the land of Juda, art not the least among the princes of Juda: for out of thee

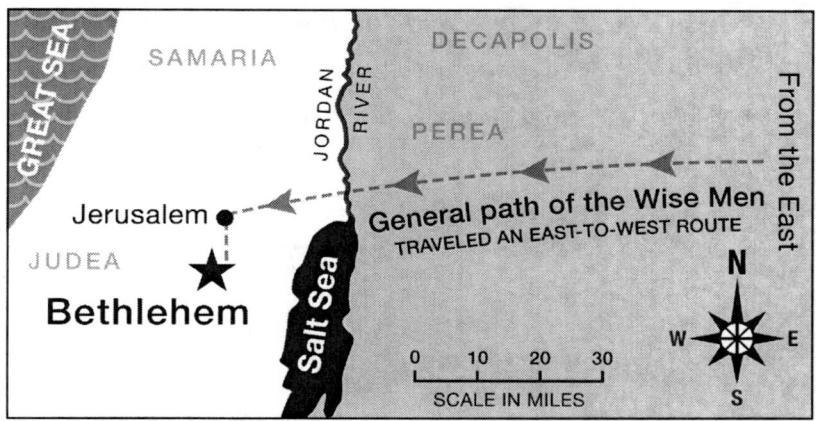

IMAGE/Jeffrey Mardis — The general route of the wise men

Because of the wording, *"we have seen his star in the east"*, and *"the star, which they saw in the east"*, many modern Christians believe that the Star of Bethlehem was an "Eastern Star". But upon closer examination, it is discovered that the word "east" is a reference to the location of the wise men – not the star (Matt. 2:1). The star was actually a western star, not an eastern star. The false teaching of the "Eastern Star" is simply another glaring example of Christians failing to compare scripture with scripture.

shall come a Governor, that shall rule my people Israel.

[7] Then Herod, when he had privily called the wise men, enquired of them diligently what time the star appeared.

[8] And he sent them to Bethlehem, and said, Go and search diligently for the young child; and when ye have found him, bring me word again, that I may come and worship him also.

[9] When they had heard the king, they departed; and, lo, the star, which they saw in the east, went before them, till it came and stood over where the young child was.

[10] When they saw the star, they rejoiced with exceeding great joy.

[11] And when they were come into the house, they saw the young child with Mary his mother, and fell down, and worshipped him: and when they had opened their treasures, they presented unto him gifts; gold, and frankincense, and myrrh.

Matthew 2:1-11

This account reveals several details and peculiarities regarding the Star.

(1) Wise men recognized that it wasn't just any star, the Star was unique, and was connected to the birth of a King...

"[1] Now when Jesus was born in Bethlehem of Judaea in the days of Herod the king, behold, there came WISE MEN from the east to Jerusalem, [2] Saying, Where is HE THAT IS BORN KING of the Jews? for we have seen HIS STAR in the east, and are come to WORSHIP HIM."   Matthew. 2:1-2

(2) The star had not always been there, but "appeared" at a specific time...

"Then Herod, when he had privily called the wise men, enquired of them diligently WHAT TIME THE STAR APPEARED." Matthew. 2:7

In contrast, considering the planet Jupiter as the Star of Bethlehem, it wasn't possible for the planet to "appear" out of nowhere and surprise the wise men as Matthew describes. Jupiter has always been visible to the unaided eye. Did you get that? In fact, Jupiter has always been one of the top most visible objects in the night sky. But don't take my word for it.

"Jupiter appears bright white and is A VERY OBVIOUS SIGHT in the night sky. Like Venus, it can be seen in twilight, and IT ALWAYS SHINES BRIGHTER THAN THE BRIGHTEST STAR in the night sky - Sirius (magnitude -1.46). Viewed from the Earth, JUPITER IS SEEN to move through about one zodiac constellation (ca. 30 degrees) EACH YEAR."[7]

"Besides the Sun, the Moon, and Venus, JUPITER IS THE BRIGHTEST OBJECT IN EARTH'S SKY, often

---

[7] Powell, Martin J . "The Naked Eye Planets in the Night Sky (and how to identify them)." . Martin J. Powell, n.d. Web. May 2014. <http://www.nakedeyeplanets. com/#jupiter>. Emphasis added.

IMAGE/Darcy O'Shea   The 2008 triple conjunction of Jupiter, Venus and the Moon

Jupiter has a regular presence in the night sky. As the image above demonstrates, it occasionally creates "conjunctions" with other celestial bodies. This is nothing new, astronomers and stargazers have observed this for centuries. Both with and without telescopes.

mistaken as a star. It is more than THREE TIMES BRIGHTER than Sirius, the brightest star."[8]

This casts doubt upon the popular Jupiter Theory. It shows that if the Star *was* Jupiter (or any other planet), there was no real reason for the wise men's excitement, regardless of the planet's encounter with other celestial events at the time (a triple conjunction with Regulus[9], and an encounter with Venus[10]). Their rejoicing and "exceeding great joy" at seeing

[8] "Jupiter." . About.com, n.d. Web. May 2014. <http://space.about.com/library/weekly/bljupiterinfo.htm>. Emphasis added.

[9] Larson, Frederick A. "A Coronation." . Frederick A. Larson, 2014. Web. May 2014. <http://www.bethlehemstar.net/starry-dance/coronation/>.

[10] Larson, Frederick A. "Westward Leading." . Frederick A. Larson, 2014. Web. May 2014. <http://www.bethlehemstar.net/starry-dance/westward-leading/>.

the star is doubtful under such circumstances. Especially if they were VIEWING A KNOWN PLANET which they were ACCUSTOMED TO SEEING at regular intervals. Why would "wise men" claim to have "seen his star", when they would have already known the event was the movement of the planet Jupiter? If the Star *was* Jupiter, and they didn't know it, they were poor stargazers (not wise men). But if the Star *wasn't* Jupiter, having suddenly "appeared", then their excitement is understandable. This is why Herod "enquired of them diligently WHAT TIME the star APPEARED".

(3) The star was not a stationary light in the sky, but a MOVING STAR which later STOPPED MOVING...

"When they had heard the king, they departed; and, lo, THE STAR, which they saw in the east, WENT BEFORE THEM, TILL IT CAME AND STOOD OVER WHERE THE YOUNG CHILD WAS. When they saw the star, they rejoiced with exceeding great joy."

Matthew 2:9-10

Note also that once the star stood still, the wise men knew exactly which house to enter (Matt. 2:9-11). This means that the star was capable of, not only leading the wise men to the cities of Jerusalem and Bethlehem in general, but also could point to the EXACT INDIVIDUAL HOUSE wherein the Saviour lay. The Bible says the Star "came and stood over where the young child was." Where was the young child? The

Bible says he was in a "house" with Joseph and Mary. At this point, the wise men rejoiced. Yet the most popular Christian study currently on this subject casts doubt on these words.

"Objects at astronomical distances cannot literally point at or selectively illuminate a specific house. However, THE IDEA THAT THE STAR POINTED THE MAGI TO A SPECIFIC HOUSE IS NOT IN THE BIBLE. It is an idea which has been ADDED to the Biblical narrative."[11]

An idea which has been added? Really? How has it been added? The Bible plainly says the star "stood over where the young child was", and the following two verses show the wise men rejoicing and entering "the house" – not simply rejoicing and entering Bethlehem (Matt. 2:9-11). Nothing's been added. This is called READING the Biblical narrative, not ADDING-TO the Biblical narrative (All good intentions aside, this is the kind of mess a Christian can get into when they choose science over scripture). This feat alone (the ability to point to a specific house), I believe, shows it to be much more advanced than any normal star. And much more advanced than any "retrograde" of the planet Jupiter.[12]

---

[11] Larson, Frederick A. "The FAQ: Frequently Asked Questions." . Frederick A. Larson, 2014. Web. May 2014. <www.bethlehemstar.net/about/faq/>. Emphasis added.

[12] AUTHOR'S NOTE: Retrograde Motion is an astronomical term which generally infers the apparent stopping and backwards motion of planets. An illusion created by the orbital path of planets in relation to observations made from earth.

IMAGE/public domain   *The Visit of the Wise Men* by Heinrich Hofmann (1900)

After following the star, the wise men arrive at the house of Jesus, Joseph and Mary. This means that the star not only had the ability to lead, but to pinpoint the exact house. Since it's impossible for astronomical phenomena to do this, Bethlehem Star theories based on astronomy must reject this fact, even though it's made plain from the text. This demonstrates that Christians should always use caution when attempting to explain the Bible with "natural" phenomena.

After leaving Jerusalem and coming "from the east", the scriptures say that the star "went before them" (it turns southward) and this is how they found the child. It's a little easier to understand how a normal star could generally lead one to a city (although the concept is kind of stretched), but to then lead one to the exact dwelling, out of hundreds or thousands of other dwellings within the same geographic location, is a miracle in itself. Practically speaking, in order to pinpoint a particular house, the star must have been much closer to the surface of the earth than any star in history. The purpose of this study is to show how this was possible.

The Time Gap

The entire journey of the wise men takes several months. For the wise men, the parameters of their journey begins in the east, when they first see the star (at or around the literal time of Christ's birth), and ends in Bethlehem when they arrive at the house of Joseph and Mary. When they first arrive at Jerusalem and speak to Herod, the babe is no longer in a stable, but a house, and by this time he is a "young child" of nearly two years. Even so, this is still considered part of the time "when Jesus was born", but it's not the very night. The scriptural chronology is as follows:

"[1] Now WHEN JESUS WAS BORN in Bethlehem of Judaea in the days of Herod the king, behold, THERE CAME wise men from the east to Jerusalem,

[7]Then Herod, when he had privily called the wise men, enquired of them diligently WHAT TIME the star appeared.

[8] And he sent them to Bethlehem, and said, Go and search diligently for THE YOUNG CHILD; and when ye have found him, bring me word again, that I may come and worship him also.

[16] Then Herod, when he saw that he was mocked of the wise men, was exceeding wroth, and sent forth, and slew all the children that were in Bethlehem, and in all the coasts thereof, from TWO YEARS OLD AND UNDER, ACCORDING TO THE TIME which he had diligently enquired of the wise men."

Matthew 2:1,7,8 & 16

At first glance, Matthew 2:1 reads like the wise men arrived in Jerusalem on the very night *"when Jesus was born"*. But further reading shows that this was not the case. This means that *a gap of time takes place* just before the first coma in Matthew 2:1. Note:

"Now when Jesus was born in Bethlehem of Judaea in the days of Herod the king..." This is the night of Christ's birth and the night the magi SEE THE STAR.

[---GAP---]

"...behold, there came wise men from the east to Jerusalem". This is some time later, no greater than two years, when the wise men finally ARRIVE AT Jerusalem.

The Bible often has gaps of time within or between verses. Matthew 2:16 helps reveal this gap. It shows that when the wise men arrived in Jerusalem, and were asked by Herod concerning "what time the star appeared", their answer was not "tonight", but probably closer to 15 - 20 months ago. For this reason, Herod later "slew all the children that were in Bethlehem...from two years old and under." The age of the children was based on the answer which Herod had "enquired of the wise men". And the additional words "and under", points to the general age of Christ; the length of the journey of the wise men; and the time which they arrived at Jerusalem in relation to when the Star first appeared. This wasn't on the exact night "when Jesus was born", but sometime under two years later.

The scriptures show that the wise men had "seen his star" while they were in the east. This seems to imply that the star stood stationary above Jerusalem (for several months)until the wise men arrived, and then it started moving to Bethlehem. But it could also be that the star lead the wise men "from the east" for hundreds of miles, and then, upon arriving at Jerusalem, turned due south towards Bethlehem. Either way, can stars do that? Can planetary alignments do that with such accuracy? I'm not talking about things barely visible to the naked eye, like the "retrograde motion" of planets, or the referencing of star charts by the ancients to slowly track celestial movements. I'm talking about something with *much more impact*, something *much more obvious* to the observer, which can point them to a single house.

An appearing star, a guiding star, a moving star, a turning star, a standing star, a pinpointing star, a unique star – what in the world is going on? In order to get the full picture, we must first step out of the book of Matthew and into the book of Luke. Many times the Bible does not reveal all of its truth in one place. Instead, to understand God's methods behind the incident, the Christian is required to study, and compare scripture with scripture. The Bible is always the best commentary on the Bible, especially for the born-again Christian (1Cor. 2:12-14). The Holy Spirit will lead us into all truth if we take heed to His words (Jn. 16:13). Studying the Bible constitutes comparing words and phrases found in the Bible, with the same words and phrases in the Bible. This is precept upon precept, and line upon line. It does not include correcting, changing or casting doubt upon the scriptures with our seminary or college educations, or using uninspired Hebrew or Greek lexicons, no matter who else we've seen do it (Gen. 3:1). If you can READ, you have the right equipment for finding the answers (Isa. 34:16). But sometimes our problem is not with the ability to READ, but with the ability to BELIEVE what we read. God's written word, the *King James Bible*, is to be received *"..not as the word of men, but as it is in truth, the word of God, which effectually worketh also in you that believe."* (1Thess. 2:13)

> *"Study to shew thyself approved unto God, a workman that needeth not to be ashamed, rightly dividing the word of truth."* 2 Timothy 2:15

> *"Whom shall he teach knowledge? and whom shall he make to understand doctrine? them that are weaned from the milk, and drawn from the breasts. For precept must be upon precept, precept upon precept; line upon line, line upon line; here a little, and there a little:"* Isaiah 28:9-10

The Heralding Angel

Also important to our study is the concurring events in the book of Luke. These events take place immediately after the birth of the Lord Jesus and fall within the SAME TIME FRAME when the wise men are on their way to Jerusalem, actively following the star, but have not yet arrived.

> *[7] And she brought forth her firstborn son, and wrapped him in swaddling clothes, and laid him in a manger; because there was no room for them in the inn.*

> *[8] And there were in the same country shepherds*

IMAGE/public domain   *The Angel and the Shepherds* by James Tissot (1886-1894)

abiding in the field, keeping watch over their flock by night.

[9] And, lo, the angel of the Lord came upon them, and the glory of the Lord shone round about them: and they were sore afraid.

[10] And the angel said unto them, Fear not: for, behold, I bring you good tidings of great joy, which shall be to all people.

[11] For unto you is born this day in the city of David a Saviour, which is Christ the Lord.

[12] And this shall be a sign unto you; Ye shall find the babe wrapped in swaddling clothes, lying in a manger.

[13] And suddenly there was with the angel a multitude of the heavenly host praising God, and saying,

[14] Glory to God in the highest, and on earth peace, good will toward men.

[15] And it came to pass, as the angels were gone away from them into heaven, the shepherds said one to another, Let us now go even unto Bethlehem, and see this thing which is come to pass, which the Lord hath made known unto us.

[16] And they came with haste, and found Mary, and Joseph, and the babe lying in a manger.

[17] And when they had seen it, they made known abroad the saying which was told them concerning this child.

[18] And all they that heard it wondered at those things which were told them by the shepherds.

[19] But Mary kept all these things, and pondered them in her heart.

[20] And the shepherds returned, glorifying and praising God for all the things that they had heard and seen, as it was told unto them.

LUKE 2:7-20

Much more will be said regarding Luke's account as the book progresses.

Chapter Summary

We now have two accounts surrounding certain events of the Christmas Story. Within this record appears the Star of Bethlehem. The interesting thing about these two accounts, is that Matthew's account mentions men being lead to the Saviour by a STAR – there's no mention of an angel doing the leading. Luke's account is just the opposite. In the book of Luke, men are being pointed to the Saviour by an ANGEL – there's no mention of a star. As a matter of fact, the word "star" (singular) appears nowhere in the 24 chapters of Luke (the plural form "stars" appears only once in Luke 21:25). While appearing unrelated on the surface, the details of these two accounts are more related than you may realize. It's obvious both accounts are addressing events which occurred at the birth of Christ. But what you may not know, is that the scriptures show a close connection between STARS and ANGELS. The next chapter will examine this relationship, and reveal in detail how the Bible, and history, uncover a link.

"O the depth of the riches both of the wisdom and knowledge of God! how unsearchable are his judgments, and his ways past finding out!" Romans 11:33

A STAR OF A DIFFERENT COLOR 4

"And the fifth angel sounded, and I saw A STAR
fall from heaven unto the earth: and TO HIM
was given the key of the bottomless pit."

Revelation 9:1

I n the previous chapter we began our study of the text regarding the Star of Bethlehem. There we reviewed the primary scriptures dealing with its appearance (Matthew 2:1-11). We also briefly looked at coinciding events in the book of Luke. At the close of the chapter we mentioned that although Matthew and Luke definitely have a general connection in regards to the birth of Christ, most

Christians perceived their accounts of the wise-men-and-the-star, and the shepherds-with-the-angel, as simply being unrelated details. A surprise came when it was announced that these "details", far from being unrelated, were actually connected. This chapter will explore how both history and the scriptures connect the two.

Stars & the Book of Revelation

One of the most obvious links between stars and angels is found in the book of Revelation.

"Write the things which thou hast seen, and the things which are, and the things which shall be hereafter; The mystery of the seven STARS which thou sawest in my right hand, and the seven golden candlesticks. The seven STARS ARE THE ANGELS of the seven churches: and the seven candlesticks which thou sawest are the seven churches." Rev. 1:19-20

This verse draws a direct connection between the two, by plainly stating that "stars are the angels". While this is focused primarily on the "angels of the seven churches", it in no way isolates these seven angels as being the only angels connected with stars. One who reads the *King James Bible* will discover that the two words are often interchangeable. Other verses in Revelation also show instances where the word "star" is used in place of "angel".

"And the fifth angel sounded, and I saw A STAR fall from heaven unto the earth: and TO HIM was given the key of the bottomless pit." Rev. 9:1

"And the STARS OF HEAVEN FELL UNTO THE EARTH, even as a fig tree casteth her untimely figs, when she is shaken of a mighty wind." Rev. 6:13

"And his tail drew the THIRD PART OF THE STARS of heaven, and did CAST THEM TO THE EARTH: and the dragon stood before the woman which was ready to be delivered, for to devour her child as soon as it was born." Rev. 12:4

Here the author of Revelation gives the personal pronoun "him" to the appearing of a "star". Revelation also mentions "stars" falling to the earth, or being cast down to the earth. To interpret these verses as being LITERAL PLANETARY BODIES renders them impossible (also see Daniel 8:10). Such things falling to the earth would destroy our planet in an instant. And for the Devil to have the ability to cast down a literal third of the celestial stars, he'd have to be many, many times larger that our galaxy. This means the earth would literally be a tiny speck when stood next to the Devil. So, no, these "stars" are not planetary stars.

Even though Revelation 1:20 makes a direct link with the words "stars" and "angels", this is actually not the Bible's strongest evidence connecting the two. The verse makes a good foundation for the doctrine, but there are several other scriptures which help strengthen the concept.

Stars & the Book of Job

In the book of Job we find the following:

> *"[4] Where wast thou when I laid the foundations of the earth? declare, if thou hast understanding. [5] Who hath laid the measures thereof, if thou knowest? or who hath stretched the line upon it? [6] Whereupon are the foundations thereof fastened? or who laid the corner stone thereof; [7] When the morning stars sang together, and all the sons of God shouted for joy?"* Job 38:4-7

In this example, we see the Lord speaking with Job. The Lord asks Job; "Where wast thou when I laid the foundations of the earth?" Answer? Job was nowhere. That being the case however, we do find a certain kind of life form present "when" the event occurred, and this special life form is singing and shouting for joy.

> *"Where wast thou WHEN I laid the foundations of the earth? ...WHEN the morning STARS sang together, and all the SONS OF GOD shouted for joy?"*

The "morning stars"? What's that? The "sons of God"? Who's that? These are both alternate titles for angels. Beings which

Job has just described as being present "when" God "laid the foundations of the earth".

Revelation and Job have not only demonstrated that the words "star" and "angel" can refer to the same thing, but other scriptures add to this connection, and show that both share several of the same characteristics.

Stars & Heavenly Hosts

Stars and angels occupy the heavens. Stars occupy the Second Heaven. Angels occupy the Third Heaven.

The phrase "stars of heaven" is used 11 times in scripture (Gen. 26:4, Ex. 32:13, Deut. 1:10, 10:22, & 28:62, Neh. 9:23, Isa. 13:10, Nah. 3:16, Mark 13:25, and Rev. 6:13 & 12:4). Of these 11 mentions, not all are speaking of tiny lights in the night sky. Instead, eight refer to PLANETARY stars, and three refer to ANGELIC stars. The title is shared.

The home of the angels is known as the "Third Heaven". It is the current location of God's Throne, a title used explicitly by the apostle Paul to describe God's dwelling place (2Cor.12:2).

"I knew a man in Christ above fourteen years ago, (whether in the body, I cannot tell; or whether out of the body, I cannot tell: God knoweth;) such an one caught UP TO THE THIRD HEAVEN. And I knew such a man, (whether in the body, or out of the body, I cannot tell: God knoweth;) How that he was caught

UP INTO PARADISE, and heard unspeakable words, which it is not lawful for a man to utter."

2 Corinthians 12:2-4

The Bible's second heaven is outer space. Although the Bible never uses the wording "second heaven", we can know that outer space may be labeled as such, due to the divisions which scripture allocates to the regions beyond planet earth. It is part of a three-tiered structure collectively known as "the heavens". Understanding the three levels of Heaven is a prime example of studying, and "rightly dividing the word of truth" (2Tim. 2:15). This triple-division of Heaven not only helps us understand how celestial, space-based planetary stars and angelic stars can both occupy the "heavens" without having to be in the exact same place, but without these divisions, the Bible's "heaven" would be a hodgepodge mess of confusing and conflicting facts.

THE FIRST HEAVEN = Sky and atmosphere surrounding the earth. Many scriptures make reference to fowl and clouds occupying the "heavens". Yet fowl and clouds do not occupy outer space. This means that PART of the "heavens" can contain clouds and living creatures, while another PART cannot. The part which cannot may be labeled as...

THE SECOND HEAVEN = Outer space. The region just beyond the earth's atmosphere is the second

IMAGE/Bigstock.com   The three levels of heaven

The Bible teaches that "Heaven" is composed of three levels. This three-part structure illustrates how stars and angels can both occupy "heaven", while at the same time, residing in different locations. Stars occupy the Second Heaven. Angels occupy the Third Heaven.

heaven. Many scriptures make reference to the sun, moon, stars and other celestial bodies occupying the "heavens". Yet no birds or clouds are present here. This is because the second heaven cannot support life, but is a DARK DEADLY REGION outside God's established dominion for man (Gen. 1:26, Isa. 45:18).

THE THIRD HEAVEN = God's dwelling place. Contrary to the common concept that God's dwelling place lies in an alternate spiritual dimension, the bible teaches no such nonsense. The region which lies BEYOND THE DARKNESS of outer space, on the other side of a giant frozen body of water (Psa. 148:4, Rev. 4:6, 15:2), is a land of light, occupied by the "Father of lights" in whom "is no darkness at all" (Jam. 1:17, 1Jn. 1:5). The scriptures label this location as "heaven", yet no sin-cursed birds, clouds, suns, moons, stars or planets dwell here. This is because the third heaven is the Home of God. It is a realm untouched by sin or darkness, and is occupied by sinless beings – like angels and other heavenly host.

Because stars and angels, each in their own special way, occupy the heavens, they can both be referred to as "heavenly host" or "host of heaven". The Christmas Story contains one of the most familiar appearances of the phrase.

"And suddenly there was with the ANGEL a multitude of the HEAVENLY HOST praising God, and saying,

Glory to God in the highest, and on earth peace, good will toward men."   Luke 2:13-14

"And he said, Hear thou therefore the word of the LORD: I saw the LORD sitting on his throne, and all the HOST OF HEAVEN standing by him on his right hand and on his left."   1Kings 22:19

Luke and 1 Kings show "host of heaven" praising God and standing by His Throne. The host which are present in these verses represent ANGELS and other heavenly beings which reside in the Third Heaven with God (like cherubim and seraphim). The fact that Luke uses the words "heavenly host" within the Christmas Story, and in context with ANGELS, is one of the first breadcrumb clues to discovering the truth behind the "star" of Bethlehem.

The exact phrase "host of heaven" is mentioned 19 times in the *King James Bible* (Deut. 4:19, 17:3, 1Kgs. 22:19, 2Kgs. 17:16, 21:3-5, 23:4-5, 2Chron. 18:18, 33:3-5, Neh. 9:6, Isa. 34:4, Jer. 8:2, 19:13, 33:22, Dan. 8:10, Zeph. 1:5, Acts 7:42). Of these 19 mentions, 15 refer to PLANETARY stars, and 4 refer to ANGELIC stars. While Luke used the phrase in connection with ANGELS, scriptures show the more common use of the phrase is in connection with STARS. Once again, the two share a title.

"Behold, I have taught you statutes and judgments, even as the LORD my God commanded me, that ye

should do so in the land whither ye go to possess it.
...And lest thou lift up thine eyes unto HEAVEN, and
when thou seest the SUN, and the MOON, and THE
STARS, even all the HOST OF HEAVEN, shouldest be
driven to worship them, and serve them, which the
LORD thy God hath divided unto all nations under
the whole heaven."   Deuteronomy 4:5&19

The "host of heaven" found in Deuteronomy shows them
in context with the sun and moon. This host is clearly a
reference to planetary-type host, and not living creatures.

In reference to the fall of Lucifer, Isaiah uses the phrase
"stars of God".

"[12] How art thou fallen from heaven, O Lucifer, son
of the morning! how art thou cut down to the ground,
which didst weaken the nations! [13] For thou hast
said in thine heart, I will ascend into heaven, I will
exalt my throne above the STARS OF GOD: I will sit
also upon the mount of the congregation, in the sides
of the north: [14] I will ascend above the heights of the
clouds; I will be like the most High."   Isaiah 14:12-14

Is Isaiah referring to planetary stars or angelic stars? Well,
at first glance it appears that it's in reference to planetary
stars. Especially with phrases like "ascend into heaven" and
"above the heights of the clouds". But I believe it would be

an oversight to omit the fact that these "stars" could equally be the angels. Satan shares his power with no one. He says; "I will ascend...I will exalt...I will sit...I will be like". He allows no room for "we". And this includes any angel that may challenge his authority or stand in his way. As a matter of fact, Revelation shows that the Devil is willing to risk war in heaven in order to defend this position. Here we see him warring against the stars of God.

> *"[7] And there was war in heaven: MICHAEL AND HIS ANGELS FOUGHT AGAINST THE DRAGON; and the dragon fought AND HIS ANGELS, [8] And prevailed not; neither was their place found any more in heaven. [9] And the great dragon was cast out, that old serpent, called the Devil, and Satan, which deceiveth the whole world: he was cast out into the earth, and HIS ANGELS were cast out WITH HIM."* Revelation 12:7-9

Here it has been demonstrated that the wording "heavenly host", "host of heaven" and "stars of God" (and other similar, yet unmentioned phrases) can all be referring to either ANGELS or PLANETARY STARS. The context will determine which of the two. Yet because one is a type and picture of the other, some scriptures, while *using a single word or phrase*, may actually be REFERRING TO BOTH AT THE SAME TIME – a verse with a double meaning (don't forget that).

Counting Stars

Stars and angels are innumerable. Modern astronomy has calculated the current number of visible stars at somewhere around 300 sextillion. Is that a real number? Supposedly. It is written as a 3 followed by 23 zeros (300,000,000,000,0 00,000,000,000). To get that large of a number you must multiply 3 trillion 100 billion times. That's a big number! But the kicker is that science is discovering more and more new stars each year. Just as recently as 2010, the star-count was *only* 100 sextillion. Today, it is at least 3 times that amount – and growing. The Lord's promise to Israel was to multiply them as the stars of heaven. This was to show Abraham, that even though he was originally childless, being 100-years-old, that the Lord could multiply his seed (Gen. 17:16-19). This is why the Lord challenged him to "tell the stars".

"And he brought him forth abroad, and said, Look now toward heaven, and TELL THE STARS, IF THOU BE ABLE TO NUMBER THEM: and he said unto him, So shall thy seed be." Genesis 15:5

"As THE HOST OF HEAVEN CANNOT BE NUMBERED, neither the sand of the sea measured: so will I multiply the seed of David my servant, and the Levites that minister unto me." Jeremiah 33:22

"Therefore sprang there even of one [Abraham], and him as good as dead, SO MANY AS THE STARS OF

IMAGE/Sweet Publishing, sweetpublishing.com   Abraham attempts to number the stars

The Lord promises to multiply the seed of Abraham innumerably, as both the sand and stars of heaven. Angels are also said to be "innumerable".

THE SKY IN MULTITUDE, and as the sand which is by the sea shore INNUMERABLE."   Hebrews 11:12

And true to form, the angels follow this pattern. Cherubims and seraphims are never mentioned in this manner, but angels are said to be "innumerable".

"...ye are come unto mount Sion, and unto the city of the living God, the heavenly Jerusalem, and to an INNUMERABLE COMPANY OF ANGELS..."

Hebrews 12:22

Shining Stars

Stars and angels can both radiate light. This is one of those kinds of points that makes many say; "I never thought of that." Well, the scriptures have, and they make it plain.

Stars radiating light:

"And God made two great lights; the greater light to rule the day, and the lesser light to rule the night: he made the STARS also. And God set them in the firmament of the heaven TO GIVE LIGHT upon the earth." Genesis 1:16-17

"For THE STARS OF HEAVEN AND THE CONSTELLATIONS thereof shall not give THEIR LIGHT: the sun shall be darkened in his going forth, and the moon shall not cause her light to shine." Isaiah 13:10

"Praise ye him, sun and moon: praise him, all ye STARS OF LIGHT." Psalms 148:3

"Thus saith the LORD, which giveth the sun for a light by day, and the ordinances of the moon and of the STARS FOR A LIGHT by night, which divideth the sea when the waves thereof roar; The LORD of hosts is his name." Jeremiah 31:35

Angels radiating light:

"And there were in the same country shepherds abiding in the field, keeping watch over their flock by night. And, lo, the ANGEL of the Lord came upon them, and the glory of the Lord SHONE ROUND ABOUT THEM: and they were sore afraid."

Luke 2:8-9

"And, behold, the ANGEL of the Lord came upon him, and A LIGHT SHINED in the prison: and he smote Peter on the side, and raised him up, saying, Arise up quickly. And his chains fell off from his hands."

Acts 12:7

"And no marvel; for Satan himself is transformed into an ANGEL OF LIGHT."   2 Corinthians 11:14

"[3] He saw in a vision evidently about the ninth hour of the day AN ANGEL of God coming in to him, and saying unto him, Cornelius. [4] And when he looked on him, he was afraid, and said, What is it, Lord? And he said unto him, Thy prayers and thine alms are come up for a memorial before God. ... [30] And Cornelius said, Four days ago I was fasting until this hour; and at the ninth hour I prayed in my house, and, behold, a man [angel] stood before me in BRIGHT CLOTHING..."   Acts 10:3-4 & 30

IMAGE/Sweet Publishing, sweetpublishing.com   "A man stood before me in bright clothing."

Light phenomena accompanies the angel seen in the vision of Cornelius, a Roman centurion which feared God and later believed on Christ.

"[1] In the end of the sabbath, as it began to dawn toward the first day of the week, came Mary Magdalene and the other Mary to see the sepulchre. [2] And, behold, there was a great earthquake: for the ANGEL of the Lord descended from heaven, and came and rolled back the stone from the door, and sat upon it. [3] HIS COUNTENANCE WAS LIKE LIGHTENING, and his raiment WHITE AS SNOW: [4] And for fear of him the keepers did shake, and became as dead men." Matthew 28:1-4

"[1] Now upon the first day of the week, very early in the morning, they came unto the sepulchre, bringing the spices which they had prepared, and certain others with them. [2] And they found the stone rolled away from the sepulchre. [3] And they entered in, and found not the body of the Lord Jesus. [4] And it came to pass, as they were much perplexed thereabout, behold, two men [angels] stood by them in SHINING GARMENTS: [5] And as they were afraid, and bowed down their faces to the earth, they said unto them, Why seek ye the living among the dead?" Luke 24:1-5

There's a classic English lullaby known as *Twinkle, Twinkle, Little Star* (c. 1806) that speaks of the shining aspect of these heavenly host. The first and fifth stanzas of the popular nursery rhyme state:

> *Twinkle, twinkle, little star,*
> *How I wonder what you are.*
> *Up above the world so high,*
> *Like a diamond in the sky.*
>
> *As your bright and tiny spark,*
> *Lights the traveller in the dark.*
> *Though I know not what you are,*
> *Twinkle, twinkle, little star.*

The word of God knows "what your are" – you are a type and picture of ANGELS!

The Secret Names of Stars

Stars and angels both have names. This link between the two is another that is not well known.

The book of Job mentions the star "Arcturus". This is the only star name found in scripture. Arcturus is found in conjunction with the star constellations of Orion, Pleiades and Mazzaroth.

> *"[2] I know it is so of a truth: but how should man be just with God? ... [8] Which alone spreadeth out the heavens, and treadeth upon the waves of the sea. [9] Which maketh ARCTURUS, ORION, and PLEIADES, and the chambers of the south. [10] Which doeth great things past finding out; yea, and wonders without number."* Job 9:2&8-10

> *"[31] Canst thou bind the sweet influences of PLEIADES, or loose the bands of ORION? [32] Canst thou bring forth MAZZAROTH in his season? or canst thou guide ARCTURUS with his sons? [33] Knowest thou the ORDINANCES OF HEAVEN? canst thou set the dominion thereof in the earth?"* Job 38:31-33

I know what you're thinking. You're thinking, how can I say that *all* the stars have names, when there's ONLY ONE NAME found in the Bible? Well, first of all, I don't believe that "Arcturus" is the name which the Lord gave to this star.

I believe the name "Arcturus" was given by man. This is because it is mentioned in context with star constellations which have names associated with mythology and false gods. This same principal is prevalent in the names of planets (Venus, Mars, Jupiter, Saturn, etc.), they're all named after false deities (except for planet Earth, of course, the Lord named this planet – Gen. 1:10). Having now said this, it means there are NO STARS MENTIONED in the Bible with names given to them by God. So how can I claim that God's given them names? Easy; because He says so.

> *"He telleth the number of the STARS; he calleth them all by THEIR NAMES."* Psalm 147:4

Yet, because of our study on the connection between stars and angels, it's obvious this verse has a *double meaning*. And the names of angels found in scripture, although far from plentiful, are a little more easily established. The Bible reveals the names of only three angels:

1.) Michael (Dan. 10:13,21 & 12:1, Jude 1:9, Rev. 12:7)
2.) Gabriel (Dan. 8:16 & 9:21, Lk. 1:19)
3.) Abaddon/Apollyon (Rev. 9:11)

So we have four names for three angels, and zero names for stars (Lucifer is not an angel, but a cherub - Ezk. 28:13-17). Four names out of *two* massive groups which God's word has defined as "innumerable". This is strange. What's going on? Regardless of the fact that both groups have names, for man, knowing these names is not important. The vast majority of these names are *secret* and only known to God. We've already shown that God has all the stars and angels *numbered* (Psa. 147:4). But has He revealed this *number* to man? No. It is simply stated that they *are* numbered, but the actual number is never disclosed. So too, God has *named* all the stars and angels. But, with the exception of the four angel names found in scripture, these names are never revealed. The book of Judges gives us insight on this matter.

> *"And Manoah said unto the ANGEL of the LORD, WHAT IS THY NAME, that when thy sayings come to pass we may do thee honour? And the ANGEL of the LORD said unto him, WHY ASKEST THOU THUS AFTER MY NAME, seeing IT IS SECRET?"* Judges 13:17-18

There are many books by modern authors which purport to tell us these names. Don't believe it. One of the most popular was written in 1994 by Gustav Davidson, and titled *A Dictionary of Angels: Including the Fallen Angels*. It is mostly an amalgam of extra-biblical information. The book's description reads:

> "Gustav Davidson's classic text, *A dictionary of Angels: Including the Fallen Angels*, is the result of sixteen years of research in Talmudic, gnostic, cabalistic, apocalyptic, patristic, and legendary texts.

The classic reference work on angels is beautifully illustrated and its reissue coincides with the resurgence of belief in angels in America. This well researched and exquisitely illustrated dictionary is a wonderful collectable for all those who believe in angels, miracles, lore, and faith."

Note that the book's description mentions a "resurgence of belief in angels in America". This "resurgence", however, has nothing to do with a resurgence in God's words, but with the rise of New Age thought (witchcraft). The Bible says; *"To the law and to the testimony: if they speak not according to this word, it is because there is no light in them."* (Isa. 8:20). Stay far, far away from books that pretend to teach something which the Bible says is "secret".

IMAGE/Internet   *A Dictionary of Angels*

Stars for Sale

Another thing related to star names, one which I've always found a little humorous, and proof that man is willing to exploit anything to make a quick buck, are organizations which claim to allow you to "officially" name stars after yourself or a loved one. This, of course, ignores the fact that the Lord has already named them (Psa. 147:4). It also requires you to PAY in order to make the name "official". There's the *International Star Registry*, *Name-A-Star*, *Memorial Star*, *Starnamer*, *Your Star Forever*, and others. Prices usually range from about $15 to $110, and usually include a "certificate of authenticity" (a piece of paper), and, for one particular company, a stuffed-animal for the kiddies. What a joke! What these businesses don't tell you, is that not only has GOD ALREADY NAMED THE STARS, but even the IAU (International Astronomical Union), the organization which regulates information on the scientific study and naming of astronomical related bodies and phenomena, does not recognize names given to stars by any of these groups. Additionally, each of these businesses keep their own private star-naming records. So the star you pick, may have already been picked and named previously, by another person who paid through a different company. Ah well, that's business.[13]

A Brief History of Fallen Stars

Because we live in a time of much deception, and false and watered-down doctrine (1Tim. 4:1, 2Tim. 3:13), and because we live in a time where a multitude of counterfeit Bible versions have changed or eliminated God's words –

---

[13] Fraser, Cain. "Can You Really Name a Star?." . *Universe Today,* 15 Aug. 2013. Web. 1 May 2014. <hhttp://www.universetoday.com/104134/can-you-really-name-a-star/>.

and generally created much confusion within the Body of Christ – many Christians today have never been aware of the close connection between stars and angels. This doesn't mean the star-angel connection is a new or recent discovery, however. Today's ignorance is merely a social commentary on the scriptural shallowness of modern Christianity. And to our shame (Hos. 4:6), much of the non-Christian world has been aware of this fact for thousands of years. Not the fact of Christian ignorance, but the fact that stars and angels have close ties.

Without going into a long, long detailed thing on this issue, a few points and reminders will suffice. Thus far, we have mainly addressed angels in the context of those which currently reside in heaven with the Lord and willfully worship and minister unto Him (the angels of God in Heaven). What we have not mentioned, however, are those angels which make up a rebellious faction and are currently in league with the Devil. While this distinction is important, it has no real bearing on the truth of the star-angel association. The reason I bring this up, is because much of the history of these FALLEN ANGELS, and specifically fallen mankind's interest in the worship of such beings, also lays bear the connections between angels and stars. For example, the FIRST FALSE GOD mentioned by name in scripture is "Molech" (Lev. 18:21 - also spelled Moloch or Malcham). Molech is a transliteration of the Hebrew word "Malak". Malak is also the Hebrew spelling for the word for "angel". In other words,

IMAGE/public domain   Giving one's seed to Molech (Lev. 18:21)

Molech is the first false god mentioned by name in scripture. The Hebrew word for Molech is "Malak", the same Hebrew word for "angel". And incidentally, the Bible connects both Molech and angels to the star symbol.

the Hebrew word for the first false god named in the Bible is spelled M-A-L-A-K[14], and the Hebrew word for "angel" is spelled M-A-L-A-K[15]. Coincidence? Not likely. Although this word connection is revealing, for the Bible reader, no such recourse to Hebrew is necessary. The scriptures themselves show that Molech is associated with the STAR SYMBOL.

---

[14] See *Strong's Concordance* Hebrew reference numbers for "Molech" - 4432, 4427

[15] See the *Strong's Concordance* Hebrew reference number for "angel" - 4397

"But ye have borne the tabernacle of your MOLOCH and Chiun your images, the STAR OF YOUR GOD, which ye made to yourselves."   Amos 5:26

"Yea, ye took up the tabernacle of MOLOCH, and the STAR OF YOUR GOD Remphan, figures which ye made to worship them: and I will carry you away beyond Babylon."   Acts 7:43

These verses also show other gods connected with the STAR SYMBOL (Chuin and Remphan), but Molech is the only one which its Hebrew root-spelling is directly comparable with the Hebrew root-spelling of angel. The bottom line is, that the roots of WITCHCRAFT are actually the origins of the WORSHIP OF FALLEN ANGELS, and the seeking-out of the forbidden wisdom which they possess. This type of worship was seeded in the days of Noah, blossomed after Noah's Flood, and later spread worldwide after the dispersal at Babel. This is the time when the world broke away from monotheism (the worship of the One true God, the Creator) and into pantheism (the worship of many gods - 1Cor. 8:5-6). Today, this ancient worship of angels and belief in many gods has also splintered into the belief in life on other planets. It is for this very reason why the most prominent symbol used in witchcraft has always been the STAR (pentagrams, hexagrams and other star-like symbols). Not only do modern occultists openly and happily use the star in their worship

IMAGE/Eliphas Levi   From the two-volume *Dogma & Ritual of High Magic* (1854-1856)

and conjuration rituals, but many make no bones regarding the fact that their guardians, or lords of the watchtowers (or whatever nonsense-name you want to call them) are, in fact, ANGELS! On the following pages are examples of how the STAR is still the most central symbol of the occult today. Although many Christians are undoubtedly aware of this, they may not have been aware of WHAT makes the symbol so important – the ancient FALLEN ANGELS.

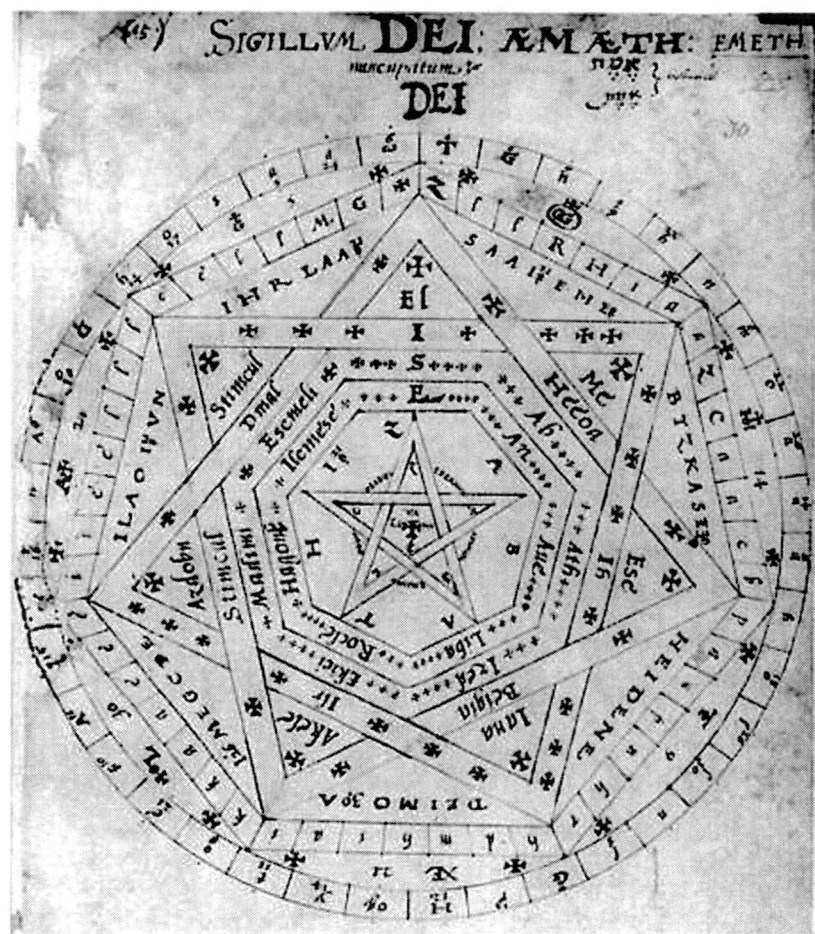

IMAGE/John Dee   Diagram of *Sigillum Dei Aemeth,* or *Seal of the Truth of God* (1582)

Sixteenth century occultists and royal astrologer to Queen Elizabeth I, John Dee (1527-1608), revised earlier versions of this occult symbol, incorporating it into his own version of angel magic (called Enochian Magic). The seal was part of a magical spoken language designed to summon and communicate with angels (note the centrality of the star symbols). The Bible never advocates such practices, but instead, associates such things with sorcery, divination, necromancy, and familiar spirits (Deut. 18:10-12). Communicating with angels is God's business, not man's business.

IMAGES/internet   A small sampling of stars found prominently in witchcraft

(Top Left) A modern pendant proclaiming "pagan family values"; (Top Right) a modern *Book of Shadows* designed for pagan altar use; (Bottom Left) a modern book teaching spells and rituals to beginners and budding witches; (Bottom Right) infamous occultist, Satanist and Freemason, Aleister Crowley (1875-1947), with the book *Perdurabo Magister*, meaning "the master that shall endure to the end".

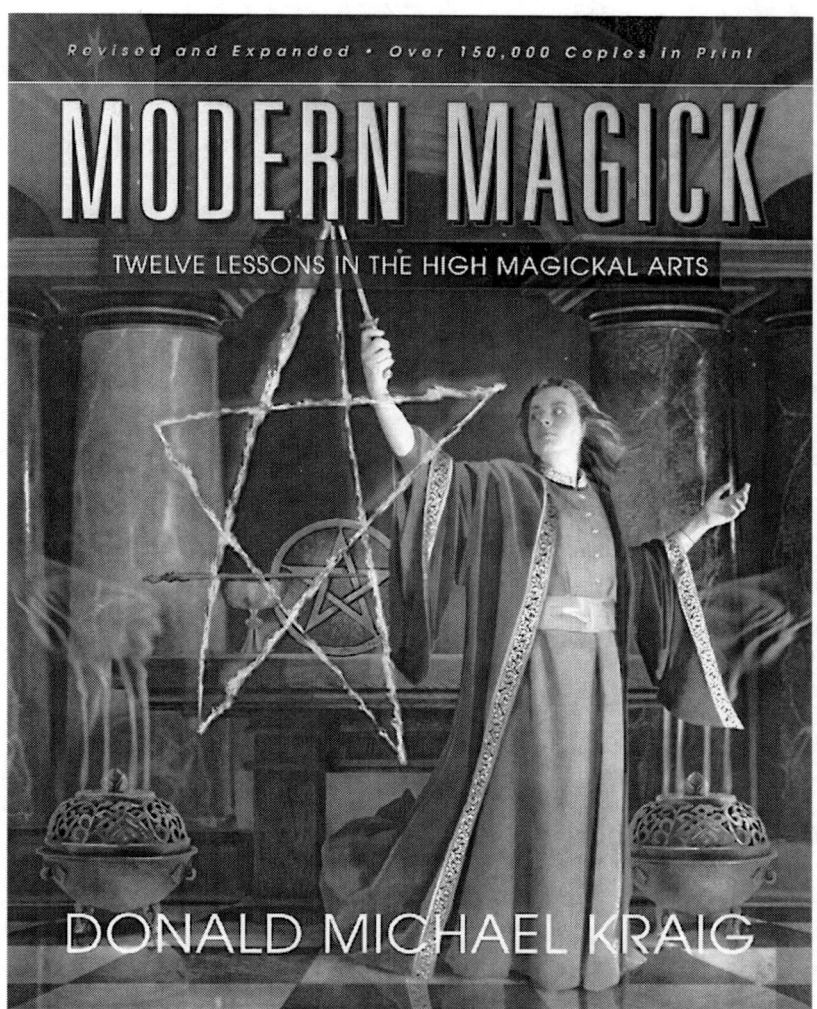

IMAGE/internet   Modern book of witchcraft

The star, in its various names and drawn forms, has always been the most important symbol of witchcraft. Because the Holy Bible is the key to all symbology, the scriptures show the star to be synonymous with angels. The same beings responsible for witchcraft's ancient origins (Gen. 6:1-4), and the source from which witchcraft admittedly receives its power today.

IMAGES/internet   Modern book Witchcraft book on angel magic

To this very day, the star symbol (pentagram or otherwise) and angels are connected with witchcraft and magical powers. That's because the fallen angels of old are responsible for inspiring the belief system (Gen. 6:1-4).

Eastern Star Ritual book
Eastern Star logo
Original Eastern Star signet designed by its founder in 1850

IMAGES/internet   Order of the Eastern Star

Freemasonry's co-Masonic group, the *Order of the Eastern Star*, also uses the pentagram extensively. The OES motto is *"We have seen his star in the east, and are come to worship him."* (Matt. 2:2). But the "Eastern Star" is not the Star of Bethlehem, regardless of how it may be depicted (see the map on page 55 for more details). The outer workings of the Masonic Lodge are used to hide the inner workings of a secret doctrine. The doctrine of the ancient Mystery Religions, and the global unity of all mankind and all religions under the headship of one god – the Antichrist.

The reason we've taken this brief rabbit trail and discussed the use of the pentagram in the centuries-old, false, anti-God religion of Witchcraft, is because this HISTORY proves the Bible to be true. It shows, just as we've covered earlier in the chapter, that STARS and ANGELS are connected, and that the STAR SYMBOL is many times used to represent ANGELS and/or the powers they represent. *God's word had already told us this*, but this historical evidence simply buttresses our findings, and shows how Witchcraft has twisted that truth into the quintessential false religion – a belief system which scripture links directly with SIN, REBELLION and REJECTION of the words of God (1Sam. 15:23).

Chapter Summary

The reason the angels and certain planetary bodies share the title of "star", is because one is a type and picture of the other. Planetary stars picture angelic stars in type. Not only did the Bible illustrate outright that angels are called "stars" (Rev. 1:20, Job 38:7, etc.), but our study also revealed that they share other words and phrases, and have four primary characteristics in common.

1 - Both occupy the heavens
2 - Both are innumerable
3 - Both emit light
4 - Both have names

Our study on the history of the worship of fallen angels also showed that the star symbol is still being used today.

An image used to represent the origin and power of the forbidden knowledge of Witchcraft – the knowledge of the fallen angels.

I believe *the connection between stars and angels holds the key to unlocking the mystery of the Star of Bethlehem.* A connection which we've identified within the Christmas Story, yet with each issue being *split* between the Gospels of Matthew and Luke. A STAR is found in Matthew, but an ANGEL is found in Luke. But our study is not over yet. By looking back at some of the details in Luke's account, details already briefly covered, I believe the final piece to the puzzle can be revealed.

"For whatsoever things were written aforetime were written for our learning, that we through patience and comfort of the scriptures might have hope." Romans 15:4

THE ANGEL OF THE LORD 5

"And the angel of the Lord appeared unto him in a flame of fire out of the midst of the bush: and ... he said, I am the God of thy father, the God of Abraham, the God of Isaac, and the God of Jacob."
Exodus 3:2&6

This chapter will focus on details presented in Luke and how those details point to the identity of the Star of Bethlehem. This information will then dovetail with Old Testament accounts of supernatural phenomena, showing how the Star aligns with signs and wonders, and the Lord's methods of dealing with Israel.

An Appearance of Angels

[7] And she brought forth her firstborn son, and wrapped him in swaddling clothes, and laid him in a manger; because there was no room for them in the inn.

[8] And there were in the same country shepherds abiding in the field, keeping watch over their flock by night.

[9] And, lo, THE ANGEL of the Lord came upon them, and the glory of the Lord shone round about them: and they were sore afraid.

[10] And THE ANGEL said unto them, Fear not: for, behold, I bring you good tidings of great joy, which shall be to all people.

[11] For unto you is born this day in the city of David a Saviour, which is Christ the Lord.

[12] And this shall be a sign unto you; Ye shall find the babe wrapped in swaddling clothes, lying in a manger.

[13] And suddenly there was with THE ANGEL a multitude of the heavenly host praising God, and saying,

IMAGE/Sweet Publishing, sweetpublishing.com   The angel of the Lord appears

When the angel of the Lord appeared unto the shepherds, the Bible says *"the glory of the Lord"* shone about them. (Luke 2:9)

[14] Glory to God in the highest, and on earth peace, good will toward men.

[15] And it came to pass, as THE ANGELS were gone away from them into heaven, the shepherds said one to another, Let us now go even unto Bethlehem, and see this thing which is come to pass, which the Lord hath made known unto us.   Luke 2:7-15

In our study thus far, we've seen that only Matthew mentions the Star of Bethlehem. Luke doesn't mention a star, but instead an appearance of angels. The Bible then goes a step further and connects the two. As demonstrated in the previous chapter, we've learned that STARS and ANGELS have much in common, including sharing the same title and phrases. So does this mean the Star of Bethlehem was an angel? Probably, but there's more.

Luke carries this connection another step further, because the book not only mentions "angels", but "the angel of the Lord" (Lk. 2:9&15). The "angel of the Lord", what's that? The Bible shows the phrase "the angel of the Lord" (or "the angel of God") can have two distinct meanings. But because of the word "of", the phrase must be read carefully, for the two different meanings can SHIFT depending upon their context. Here are the two possible meanings:

MEANING #1 - The phrase "the angel of the Lord" or "the angel of God" may refer to ANY ANGEL that comes from the Lord or that belongs to the Lord (like Michael or Gabriel). This meaning draws a distinction from angels that may be "of the Devil". There are angels "of the Lord", and angels "of the Devil" (see Rev. 12:9).

MEANING #2 - The phrase "the angel of the Lord" or "the angel of God" may refer to THE ANGEL that IS God. Not just an angel that serves the Lord (like Michael or Gabriel), but an angel that IS the Lord. A literal appearance "of the Lord" Himself, under the guise of an angel.

Of these two meanings, the words of Luke point to MEANING #2 as being the kind of angel which announces the Saviour's birth. How do we know this? Because the details show that when the angel appeared "the glory of the Lord" shines round about the shepherds – not the glory of an angel. The news of Christ's birth is also announced from the mouth of this same angel. Immediately following this proclamation the shepherds testify;

> *"Let us now go even unto Bethlehem, and see this thing which is come to pass, which THE LORD HATH MADE KNOWN UNTO US."* Luke 2:15

Even thought the shepherds had just witnessed "a multitude of heavenly host", none of them professed that "angels" were responsible for the announcement. Isn't that strange? They singled-out *"the Lord"* as announcing the revelation. Why is this significant? Because these verses now connect Luke's "angel of the Lord" with GOD'S GLORY and GOD'S VOICE. A connection which the Bible made, between God and a special kind of "angel", centuries before.

The Angel that Speaks with God's Voice

The following scripture marks the first appearance of the phrase "the angel of God":

"[17] And God heard the voice of the lad; and THE ANGEL OF GOD called to Hagar out of heaven, and SAID unto her, What aileth thee, Hagar? fear not; for GOD HATH HEARD the voice of the lad where he is. [18] Arise, lift up the lad, and hold him in thine hand; for I WILL MAKE HIM A GREAT NATION."

Genesis 21:17-18

Here the Bible shows that this angel represents the same personality which would make Ishmael into a nation. Note especially the use of the pronoun (first person singular) "I";

"...the angel of God...said...I will make him a great nation."

No regular angel has the power or ability to do this. Michael can't make Ishmael a great nation. Gabriel can't make Ishmael a great nation. This shows that the *first mention* of "the angel of God" means "the angel [that is] God".

Interestingly, while Luke shows "the angel of the Lord" appearing at the BIRTH of Christ, the Old Testament shows "the angel of the Lord" appearing at the BIRTH of the nation of Israel. Did you get that? A special kind of angel appearing at two events which God identifies as His "son".

"And the Word was made flesh, and dwelt among us, (and we beheld his glory, the glory as of THE ONLY BEGOTTEN OF THE FATHER,) full of grace and

truth. ... For God so loved the world, that he gave HIS ONLY BEGOTTEN SON, that whosoever believeth in him should not perish, but have everlasting life."

John 1:14 & 3:16, et. al

"[21] And the LORD said unto Moses, When thou goest to return into Egypt, see that thou do all those wonders before Pharaoh, which I have put in thine hand: but I will harden his heart, that he shall not let the people go. [22] And thou shalt say unto Pharaoh, Thus saith the LORD, ISRAEL IS MY SON, even my firstborn: [23] And I say unto thee, LET MY SON GO, that he may serve me: and if thou refuse to let him go, behold, I will slay thy son, even thy firstborn."

Exodus 4:21-23

"[2] And THE ANGEL OF THE LORD appeared unto him in a flame of fire OUT OF THE MIDST OF THE BUSH: and he looked, and, behold, the bush burned with fire, and the bush was not consumed. [3] And Moses said, I will now turn aside, and see this great sight, why the bush is not burnt. [4] And when THE LORD saw that he turned aside to see, GOD CALLED UNTO HIM OUT OF THE MIDST OF THE BUSH, and said, Moses, Moses. And he said, Here am I. [5] And he said, Draw not nigh hither: put off thy shoes from off thy feet, for the place whereon thou standest

IMAGE/Sweet Publishing, sweetpublishing.com   The angel of the Lord appears to Moses

When the angel of the Lord appeared unto Moses in the burning bush, the Bible says that Moses *"was afraid to look upon God"*. (Exodus 3:6)

is holy ground. [6] Moreover he said, I AM THE GOD OF THY FATHER, the God of Abraham, the God of Isaac, and the God of Jacob. And Moses hid his face; for he was afraid TO LOOK UPON GOD."

Exodus 3:2-6

Exodus tells first of the ANGEL of the Lord appearing "out of the midst of the bush", and then it shows GOD speaking "out of the midst of the bush". It's *an angel speaking with God's voice*. After Israel is lead out of Egypt, this same angel appears again.

"[20] Behold, I send an Angel before thee, to keep thee in the way, and to bring thee into the place which I have prepared. [21] BEWARE OF HIM, and OBEY HIS VOICE, PROVOKE HIM NOT; for he will not PARDON YOUR TRANSGRESSIONS: for MY NAME IS IN HIM. [22] But if thou shalt indeed OBEY HIS VOICE, and do all that I SPEAK; then I will be an enemy unto thine enemies, and an adversary unto thine adversaries. [23] For MINE Angel shall GO BEFORE THEE, and bring thee in unto the Amorites, and the Hittites, and the Perizzites, and the Canaanites, the Hivites, and the Jebusites: and I will cut them off." Exodus 23:20-23

These verses teach 7 profound facts regarding this special kind of angel:

1.) It's an angel with a capital "A"
2.) God calls this angel "mine Angel"
3.) It's an angel which can pardon transgressions
4.) God's name is "in" this angel
5.) God connects His words to this angel's voice
6.) Israel is commanded to obey this angel's voice
7.) It's a leading and guiding angel

Genesis identifies the angel with the capital "A" as God, the redeeming "Angel".

"[15] And he blessed Joseph, and said, GOD, before whom my fathers Abraham and Isaac did walk, THE GOD which fed me all my life long unto this day, [16] THE ANGEL WHICH REDEEMED ME FROM ALL EVIL, bless the lads; and let my name be named on them, and the name of my fathers Abraham and Isaac; and let them grow into a multitude in the midst of the earth." Genesis 48:15-16

Additionally, the phrase "mine Angel" appears three times in scripture. Its first and second mention are both in Exodus, and both connect the Angel to the leading and guiding of people to a specific location.

"And the LORD said unto Moses, Whosoever hath sinned against me, him will I blot out of my book. Therefore now go, LEAD THE PEOPLE unto the place of which I have spoken unto thee: behold, MINE Angel SHALL GO BEFORE THEE..." Ex. 32:33-34

Both accounts in Exodus testify that; "...mine Angel shall go before thee..." (Ex. 23:23 & 32:34). So how do the scriptures describe this angel of the Lord – this angel with the capital "A" – going before Israel and leading them?

Angel of the Elements

The Old Testament reveals that one of the jobs of the angel of the Lord was to lead and guide God's people. This leading and guiding was accomplished through a very peculiar ability. The ability for the angel to appear, not as a man (the customary appearance of angels in the Bible), but as ELEMENTS OF NATURE.

"And THE LORD WENT BEFORE THEM by day in a pillar of a CLOUD, TO LEAD THEM THE WAY; and by night in a pillar of FIRE, to give them LIGHT; to go by day and night"   Exodus 13:21

"[13] And Moses said unto the LORD, Then the Egyptians shall hear it, (for thou broughtest up this people in thy might from among them;) [14] And they will tell it to the inhabitants of this land: for they have heard that thou LORD art among this people, that thou LORD art seen face to face, and that THY CLOUD STANDETH OVER THEM, and that THOU GOEST BEFORE THEM, by day time in a pillar of a CLOUD, and in a pillar of FIRE BY NIGHT."   Numbers 14:13-14

"[32] Yet in this thing ye did not believe the LORD your God, [33] Who WENT IN THE WAY BEFORE YOU, to search you out a place to pitch your tents in, IN FIRE by night, TO SHEW YOU BY WHAT WAY YE SHOULD GO, and IN A CLOUD by day."   Deuteronomy 1:32-33

IMAGE/Sweet Publishing, sweetpublishing.com   The angel of the Lord appears as a cloud

When the angel of the Lord appeared to the nation of Israel, He lead them via the elemental form of a pillar of cloud and fire. (Exodus 13:21, etc.)

"Moreover THOU LEDDEST THEM in the day by a CLOUDY PILLAR; and in the night by a pillar of FIRE, TO GIVE THEM LIGHT IN THE WAY WHEREIN THEY SHOULD GO."   Nehemiah 9:12

Additionally, these special elemental, nature-like, "angel of the Lord" manifestations, not only lead and guide, but also can stop and stand still in very specific and precise locations.

"And THE ANGEL OF GOD, which WENT BEFORE the camp of Israel, removed and WENT BEHIND

them; and the pillar of the CLOUD WENT FROM BEFORE their face, and STOOD BEHIND them."

Exodus 14:19

"And THE SIGHT OF THE GLORY OF THE LORD was like DEVOURING FIRE ON THE TOP OF THE MOUNT in the eyes of the children of Israel."

Exodus 24:17

"And it came to pass, as Moses entered into the tabernacle, the CLOUDY PILLAR descended, and STOOD at the door of the tabernacle, and the LORD talked with Moses."   Exodus 33:9

"And THE LORD CAME DOWN in the pillar of the CLOUD, and STOOD in the door of the tabernacle, and called Aaron and Miriam: and they both came forth."   Numbers 12:5

"And THE LORD APPEARED in the tabernacle in a pillar of a CLOUD: and the pillar of the cloud STOOD over the door of the tabernacle."   Deuteronomy 31:15

Exodus, Numbers, Deuteronomy and Nehemiah all show the angel of the Lord leading God's people through a pillar of cloud and fire. Even though these are said to be ANGELIC, ELEMENTAL manifestations (clouds and fire), the scriptures say "the Lord went before them" and "thou goest before them" and "God, who went in the way before you", and "thou leddest them". Did you get that? Yet these are not natural phenomena guided by God's ordinances (like rain clouds, tornados or firenados). We're dealing with something much, much more here. These are SUPERNATURAL EVENTS connected with God's Person. Events which have no real scientific explanation, and appear as ELEMENTS OF NATURE that operate OUTSIDE THE LAWS OF NATURE. They are special signs and wonders from God.

Chapter Summary

This chapter has focused on Luke's account of Christ's birth. From that Christmas event, we learned of "the angel of the Lord" and the circumstances which surrounded his appearance. While the Bible shows that "the angel of the Lord" may be ANY ANGEL from Heaven (like Michael or Gabriel), we discovered that a special kind of "Angel" appeared in Old Testament times and helped lead Israel out of bondage by means of a supernatural pillar of cloud and fire. This special kind of Angel, which the Lord God called "mine Angel", could pardon transgressions and had God's name "in him" (Ex. 23:21). Was this the Archangel Michael? No. Michael couldn't pardon transgression, for as the scribes and Pharisees once said; *"Who can forgive sins, but God alone?"* (Luke 5:21). And God's name is not "in" Michael. But God's name is in the One who was manifest in the flesh, on the night of the appearance of the Star of Bethlehem. The

One who is called *"Emmanuel, which being interpreted is, GOD WITH US."* (Matt. 1:23). The next chapter will conclude our study, and show how the scriptures conclusively link the Star of Bethlehem to an appearance of the Lord Jesus Christ Himself.

"The entrance of thy words giveth light; it giveth understanding unto the simple"

Psalms 119:130

THE STAR IDENTIFIED 6 ✺

> *"... Where is he that is born King of the Jews?*
> *for we have seen HIS STAR in the east,*
> *and are come to worship him."*
> Matthew 2:2

Was the Star of Bethlehem the angel of the Lord, a veiled appearance of the Lord Jesus Christ? While such a statement may sound like a stretch, the scriptural evidence accumulated at this point should at least give one room for pause. Here's a partial rundown of some of the parallels and "coincidences" we've discovered in our study thus far:

1.) Matthew testifies of a star which lead men to Christ.

2.) Luke testifies of an angel which pointed men to Christ.

3.) The Bible connects stars with angels

4.) History connects stars with angels

5.) Luke reveals this angel was "the angel of the Lord".

6.) Luke's angel of the Lord shined forth "the glory of the Lord".

7.) Exodus' angel of the Lord helped lead and guide.

8.) Matthew's star helped lead and guide.

9.) Exodus' angel of the Lord appears when God's national "son" is born (Israel).

10.) Matthew's star appears when God's "only begotten Son" is born (Jesus - God in the Flesh).

11.) Exodus shows God calling the angel of the Lord "mine Angel".

12.) This Angel had the power to pardon transgressions.

13.) God claimed His name was "in" this Angel.

Because, neither the angels of God in heaven, nor Satan's angels, meet all these qualifications they are easily eliminated. This narrows the field considerably. Since the Lord says of this Angel that "my name is in him" (Ex. 23:21) and "Emmanuel, which being interpreted is, GOD WITH US" (Matt. 1:23) was born on the night of Bethlehem's Star, we now have ample reason to explore the connection that Christ Jesus is the Star.

The Angel that Paul Served

In the last chapter of Revelation, John is so full of awe that he falls at the feet and worships the messenger who's shown him the future and the stunning things to come. An act for which he's rebuked.

> *"[8] And I John saw these things, and heard them. And when I had heard and seen, I FELL DOWN TO WORSHIP before the feet of the ANGEL which shewed me these things. [9] Then saith he unto me, SEE THOU DO IT NOT: for I am thy FELLOWSERVANT, and of thy brethren the prophets, and of them which keep the sayings of this book: WORSHIP GOD."*
>
> Revelation 22:8-9

This incident shows that the angels of God in heaven DO NOT ACCEPT WORSHIP. And not only that, if you attempt to worship them, they will immediately point you to the only One worthy of worship – GOD. Knowing this, we find the

Apostle Paul making mention of a peculiar kind of angel. Compare Paul's words with Joshua's words.

"For there stood by me this night THE ANGEL OF GOD, WHOSE I AM, and WHOM I SERVE"

Acts 27:23

"And if it seem evil unto you to serve the LORD, CHOOSE YOU THIS DAY WHOM YE WILL SERVE; whether the gods which your fathers served that were on the other side of the flood, or the gods of the Amorites, in whose land ye dwell: but as for me and my house, WE WILL SERVE THE LORD"

Joshua 24:15

Did Paul belong to an angel? Did Paul serve an angel? No, not the kind of angel that we usually think of. Note in the following verse how Paul makes a parallel reference to the identity of the "angel" whom he professed to serve.

"And my temptation which was in my flesh ye despised not, nor rejected; but received me as an ANGEL OF GOD, even as CHRIST JESUS."

Galatians 4:14

This scripture demonstrates that this "angel of God", IS God, even the Lord Jesus Christ. This is why God states in Exodus that His name is "in him", and commanded Israel to "beware of him", and "obey his voice", and that the angel would not "pardon" their transgressions if they refused to do so. This Angel could not only speak the words of God, but IS "the Word of God".

> *"In the beginning was the Word, and the Word was with God, and the Word was God. ... And the Word was made flesh, and dwelt among us, (and we beheld his glory, the glory as of the only begotten of the Father,) full of grace and truth."* 1John 1&14

These words of Paul, inspired by the Holy Spirit, directly link the Lord Jesus Christ to "the angel of God" or "the angel of the Lord". This link also means that any manifestations of *this* angel apply to Jesus Christ. Particularly revealing in our case, are the appearances of the angel of the Lord in the form of pillars of cloud and fire. They show that CHRIST CAN TAKE ON THE APPEARANCE OF NATURE-LIKE PHENOMENA. After all, one of the Bible's most consistent descriptive pictures of God shows that HE IS LIGHT and a CONSUMING FIRE. This light is not only present in the form of SPIRITUAL LIGHT (truth), but in the form of LITERAL LIGHT. A kind of Light *different* from created light (sun, moon, stars, etc.). The kind of light which has been ETERNALLY PRESENT IN GOD even before the creation of the universe (Gen. 1:1). Note how the following scriptures show the Lord as both literal Light and spiritual Light.

"This then is the message which we have heard of him, and declare unto you, that GOD IS LIGHT, and in him is no darkness at all."   1John 1:5

"[6] There was a man sent from God, whose name was John. [7] The same came for a witness, to bear witness of THE LIGHT, that all men through him might believe. [8] He was not THAT LIGHT, but was sent to bear witness of THAT LIGHT. [9] That was the TRUE LIGHT, which lighteth every man that cometh into the world. [10] He [the Lord Jesus Christ] *was in the world, and the world was made by him, and the world knew him not."*   John 1:6-10

"The sun shall be no more thy light by day; neither for brightness shall the moon give light unto thee: but THE LORD SHALL BE UNTO THEE AN EVERLASTING LIGHT, and thy God thy glory."
                    Isaiah 60:19

"And the city [New Jerusalem] *had NO NEED OF THE SUN, neither of the moon, TO SHINE IN IT: for THE GLORY OF GOD DID LIGHTEN IT, and THE LAMB IS THE LIGHT thereof."*   Revelation 21:23

"For our God is a consuming FIRE."   Hebrews 12:29

A Light Brighter than the Sun

Before Paul's conversion, he encountered an amazing phenomenon on the road to Damascus. This supernatural encounter forever alters the course of his life.

> *"[3] And as he journeyed, he came near Damascus: and suddenly THERE SHINED ROUND ABOUT HIM A LIGHT FROM HEAVEN: [4] And he fell to the earth, and heard A VOICE saying unto him, Saul, Saul, why persecutest thou me? [5] And he said, Who art thou, Lord? And THE LORD SAID, I AM JESUS whom thou persecutest: it is hard for thee to kick against the pricks."*   Acts 9:3-5

Paul again testifies of this life-changing event on two occasions.

> *"[6] And it came to pass, that, as I made my journey, and was come nigh unto Damascus ABOUT NOON, suddenly THERE SHONE FROM HEAVEN A GREAT LIGHT ROUND ABOUT ME. [7] And I fell unto the ground, and heard A VOICE saying unto me, Saul, Saul, why persecutest thou me? [8] And I answered, Who art thou, Lord? And he said unto me, I AM JESUS OF NAZARETH, whom thou persecutest. [9] And they that were with me SAW INDEED THE LIGHT, and were afraid; but they heard not THE VOICE of him that spake to me."*   Acts 22:6-9

"[12] Whereupon as I went to Damascus with authority and commission from the chief priests, [13] AT MIDDAY, O king, I saw in the way A LIGHT FROM HEAVEN, ABOVE THE BRIGHTNESS OF THE SUN, SHINNING ROUND ABOUT ME and them which journeyed with me. [14] And when we were all fallen to the earth, I heard A VOICE speaking unto me, and saying in the Hebrew tongue, Saul, Saul, why persecutest thou me? it is hard for thee to kick against the pricks. [15] And I said, Who art thou, Lord? And he said, I AM JESUS whom thou persecutest."   Acts 26:12-15

"I am Jesus", "I am Jesus", "I am Jesus". Did you get that? This light, which appears "at midday" and is "above the brightness of the sun", is connected to Christ Himself. The ability for LIGHT PHENOMENA to be present during the day and to be a significant factor, apart from the light of the sun, is also a requirement of the Star of Bethlehem. This light is obviously manifest when the angel of the Lord appears to the shepherds at NIGHT. But Paul's super-light, which appears "at midday", is just the kind of light needed for a "star" to lead wise men on a trip lasting several days AND nights. A natural celestial star cannot adequately fulfill this need, especially during the daytime hours. But Christ as the angel of the Lord CAN. This adds even more scriptural weight to the theory that the wise men followed the Light of

IMAGE/public domain   *Conversion of Paul* by Nicolas Bernard Lepicie (1767)

When Christ appears to Saul (Paul) on the road to Damascus, the Lord's presence is manifest as a light brighter than the noon-day sun.

the Son, and not the light of a sun. In more ways than one, Christ is the "day star" (2 Peter 1:19).

The Transfiguration

"[1] And after six days JESUS taketh Peter, James, and John his brother, and bringeth them up into an high mountain apart, [2] And was transfigured before them: and his face did SHINE AS THE SUN, and his raiment was WHITE AS THE LIGHT."

Matthew 17:1-2

"[2] And after six days JESUS taketh with him Peter, and James, and John, and leadeth them up into an high mountain apart by themselves: and he was transfigured before them. [3] And his raiment became SHINING, EXCEEDING WHITE as snow; so as no fuller on earth can white them." Mark 9:2-3

"[29] And as he prayed, the fashion of his countenance was altered, and his raiment was WHITE AND GLISTERING. [30] And, behold, there talked with him two men, which were Moses and Elias: [31] Who appeared in glory, and spake of his decease which he should accomplish at Jerusalem. [32] But Peter and they that were with him were heavy with sleep: and when they were awake, THEY SAW HIS GLORY, and the two men that stood with him." Luke 9:29-32

Note that Luke's record of the Lord's transfiguration states that "they saw his glory". When cross-referenced with Matthew and Mark, we see this glory appearing as white, shinning light. Since we've now connected the angel of the Lord with Christ, and also read of the circumstances surrounding Paul's conversion, it's easy to see why this evidence slides hand-in-glove with "the glory of the Lord" which shined around the shepherds.

> *"And, lo, THE ANGEL OF THE LORD came upon them, and THE GLORY OF THE LORD shone round about them: and they were sore afraid."*   Luke 2:9

The First & Last Star

In chapter 4 we covered four points which demonstrated why the scriptures use the words "star" and "angel" interchangeably. The primary reason for this is that *one is a type and picture of the other*. Of those points, the emission of light was the sole physical characteristic shared between the two. Since the Lord Jesus Christ is often referred to as an "angel" (the angel of the Lord or the angel of God), then it's reasonable to assume that he would fulfill this characteristic as well. And he does. God is Light. These similarities also imply that Christ, in some way, is also linked to the word "star".

The word "star" (singular) is used in 14 scriptures. The very first reference to the singular tense of the word is found in the book of Numbers.

> *"I shall see him, but not now: I shall behold him, but not nigh: there shall come a STAR OUT OF JACOB,*

and a Sceptre shall rise out of Israel, and shall smite
the corners of Moab, and destroy all the children of
Sheth."   Numbers. 24:17

This is interesting. Why? Because not only does this FIRST MENTION of the word have a capital "S" (Star), but it's in reference to a PERSON and not a celestial body like a star, sun or planet. Think about it. This Star refers to a King that shall arise "out of Jacob" (that's the symbology of the "Sceptre" – a ruling king with a kingdom).

"But unto THE SON he saith, THY THRONE, O GOD,
is for ever and ever: a SCEPTRE of righteousness is
the SCEPTRE of thy kingdom."   Hebrews 1:8

This rising Sceptre is why Herod was "troubled" (Matt. 2:3). It created a threat to his authority. In an effort to eliminate this threat, Herod had all the children murdered "from two years old and under" (Matt. 2:16). In other words, just as the nativity story tells of a "King" which shall rise out of "Bethlehem" (Matt. 2:2), so too, the book of Numbers relates the rise of a "Star out of Jacob". This "Star" is the Lord Jesus Christ. That's why the word is capitalized. JESUS CHRIST THE STAR. *Isn't it interesting that the Bible compares Christ's birth to the coming of a Star, when such a phenomena appeared in the sky on the VERY NIGHT of His birth?* Coincidence? I don't think so. Was the star which lead the wise men on the night of Christ's birth A DIFFERENT

STAR than the Star prophesied to "come out of Jacob" on the SAME NIGHT? Again, I don't think so. The scriptures show that Christ can easily do BOTH (i.e. incarnate Himself as a baby in a manger, and appear as a guiding Light in the sky). I believe the coming of this Star is true in more ways than one. *It prophesied of Christ as a rising King AND a rising Star.* And that's not all, the Bible's last reference to the word "star" reveals:

"I Jesus have sent MINE ANGEL to testify unto you these things in the churches. I AM THE root and the offspring of David, and the bright and morning STAR." Revelation 22:16

While this star does not have a capital "S", the Lord Jesus Christ is claiming it nonetheless. His words are unmistakable: "I am the...star". And in this case, the "day star", or "bright and morning star". A Star which can manifest a Light "above the brightness of the sun" (as the Apostle Paul testifies in Acts 26:13), and one which can literally shine a beam round about whomever it chooses (Lk. 2:9, Acts 9:3, 22:6 & 26:13). In the Old Testament, God refers to this Star as "mine Angel" (Ex. 23:23 & 32:34), here we see the Bible's last reference to the words "mine angel", and we learn that it is an appearance of CHRIST connected with a STAR. The FIRST Bible reference to the word "Star" is a reference to Christ, and the LAST Bible reference to the word "star" is a reference to Christ (Num. 24:17, Rev. 22:16). THE LORD JESUS CHRIST IS THE FIRST AND LAST STAR. He is the angel with the capital "A", and the star with the capital "S". Angels are likened unto stars, and the Lord Jesus Christ is likened unto a Star. This means that (get it now) NOT ALL STARS ARE EQUAL. There are good stars, bad stars, and there's God's Star. There are good angels, bad angels, and there's God's Angel. There are the angels of God in heaven, Satan's fallen angels, and there's the Lord Jesus Christ. All can be TYPIFIED BY THE SAME SYMBOLOGY, but they're not all the same *"...for one star differeth from another star in glory."* (1Cor. 15:41)

When all these pieces are put together (all the information from the previous chapters), you're strongly pushed towards the conclusion that *the Star of Bethlehem was actually a veiled appearance of the Lord Jesus Christ.* If this is true, it means that Christ is the missing link between Matthew's star and Luke's angel. He is the thread which ties the two Christmas accounts together even more so than before. The Old Testament appearances of pillars of cloud and fire demonstrate that THE LORD HIMSELF CAN MANIFEST AS NATURE-LIKE PHENOMENA. The Bible connects this phenomena with "the angel of the Lord". An angel which at times appears, not as a man, but as natural elements like cloud, fire or light. The SAME WORDS used by Luke to describe the angel which shined "the glory of the Lord" round about the shepherds.

Mysterious Appearances of God

The proposition that the Star of Bethlehem may be a veiled appearance of the Lord Jesus Christ may, at first, sound unorthodox. But such diverse appearances of the Godhead are common in scripture. *God can manifest Himself in any form He wishes.* In theological circles this ability is known as a "Theophany" (thee-OFF-uh-nee) or a "Christophany" (kri-STOFF-uh-nee). Terms used to help organize and compartmentalize doctrine. The Bible shows that these unique appearances of the Godhead can be manifested in four different forms. Strange? Yes. But true.

1.) APPEARANCES OF THE GODHEAD IN HUMAN FORM - When manifest in this type appearance, the Lord looks like a "man". Examples include Melchizadek (Gen. 14:18 & Heb. 7:1-3); the Captain of the Lord's Host (Josh. 5:13-15); the man that promises Abraham a son and warns of Sodom and Gomorrah's destruction (Gen. 18:1-33); and the man who wrestles with Jacob (Gen. 32:24-32). These particular appearances of God as a "man" exclude "the man Christ Jesus" (1Tim. 2:5). The Lord Jesus Christ is unique among God's "man" appearances, for He, being the second member of the Godhead, is *"the express image of his person"* (Heb. 1:3 - more on this at the close of this section).

IMAGE/Sweet Publishing, sweetpublishing.com   Three men visit Abraham

When Abraham is visited by three "men", the Bible reveals that one man is the Lord, and the other two are the angels who rescued Lot from the destruction of Sodom. (Gen. 18 & 19)

2.) APPEARANCES OF THE GODHEAD IN NATURE FORM - When manifest in this type appearance, the Lord looks like natural phenomena. Light, clouds and fire are some of the most outstanding examples of this type form. God even claims to *be* Light and a "consuming fire" (1Jn 1:5, Heb, 12:29). Many verses demonstrate the Lord's close connection with FIRE. The first time the word "fire" appears in scripture, it's coming "from the Lord out of heaven" (Gen. 19:24). When God first appears to the nation

IMAGE/Sweet Publishing, sweetpublishing.com   Elijah and the prophets of Baal

The prophet Elijah said to the prophets of Baal, that *"the God that answereth by fire"* is the true God. This is because God is both light, and a consuming fire. (1Kings 18:24)

of Israel, He appears as *fire* out of a bush (Ex. 3:2-4). When God leads Israel in their flight from Egypt, He appears as a pillar of cloud and *fire*. When God appears to Israel at Sinai, He appears as *fire* upon the mount (Ex. 19:18, 24:17, Deut. 5:4, etc.). When Elijah challenged the 450 prophets of Baal, he stated;

"And call ye on the name of your gods, and I will call on the name of the LORD: and THE GOD THAT ANSWERETH BY FIRE, let him be God." 1Kgs. 18:24

3.) APPEARANCES OF THE GODHEAD IN ANGEL FORM - Known as "the angel of the Lord" or "the angel of God", when manifest in this type appearance, the Lord looks like an angel. What do angels look like? They look exactly like *men* (this includes having no wings). In fact, the Bible shows such a close relationship between the physical appearance of angels and the physical appearance of men, that the words are often used interchangeably. Numerous examples of this can be found throughout scripture (Gen. 16:7-8, Gen. 19:1-16, Num. 22:22-35, Jud. 6:11-21, Jud. 13:2-21, 1Chron. 21:16, Matt. 28:2-6, Mk. 16:2-7, Acts 10:2-4, etc.) In other words, angels are indistinguishable from human males. It is for this reason that some have "entertained angels unawares" (Heb. 13:2).

Other scriptures show that when the Lord appears as an angel, the angel can look like *natural phenomena* (Ex. 3:2, 14:19, Acts 7:30, etc.). This means the Godhead can manifest as an ANGEL and look like a MAN (Gen. 48:16), or the Godhead can manifest as a ANGEL and look like an element of NATURE – a single appearance of the Godhead as an "angel", using multiple descriptive terms (man, fire, etc.). *This use of multiple names for a single appearance, is key to understanding our study regarding the Star of Bethlehem.* It shows that Christ Himself could have

IMAGE/Sweet Publishing, sweetpublishing.com   A pillar of fire leading Israel

When Israel became a nation, God's Angel helped lead them out of Egypt, under the appeared of a pillar of fire. (Exodus 13:21, etc.)

easily been the Presence behind the phenomena, while simultaneously being identified as an "angel" (Lk. 2:9) and a "star" (Matt. 2:2). It is simply another example of a single appearance of the Godhead, using multiple descriptive terms.[16]

4.) APPEARANCES OF THE GODHEAD IN ANIMAL FORM - When manifest in this type

---

[16] AUTHOR'S NOTE: Isaiah 63:9 even identifies God's angel as *"the angel of his presence"*.

IMAGE/Sweet Publishing, sweetpublishing.com   The Holy Spirit descends on Christ

At Christ's baptism, the Holy Spirit takes on *"the bodily shape"* of a dove. God manifesting in animal form is very rare. (Luke 3:22)

appearance, the Lord looks like an animal. This is very rare. But the scriptures are clear. Only two appearance of the Lord show Him in animal form. Luke describes the Holy Spirit appearing as a dove.

"And the Holy Ghost descended IN A BODILY SHAPE LIKE A DOVE upon him, and a voice came from heaven, which said, Thou art my beloved Son; in thee I am well pleased."   Luke 3:22

John describes literally seeing the appearance of a lamb in heaven.

"And I BEHELD, and, lo, in the midst of the throne and of the four beasts, and in the midst of the elders, stood A LAMB as it had been slain, having seven horns and seven eyes, which are the seven Spirits of God sent forth into all the earth." Revelation 5:6

I've tried to be very careful in explaining how God can manifest in these forms, while equally upholding the sanctity and holiness of the Trinity. Care must be taken in rightly dividing the scriptures. The bottom line is, like the triune Godhead, this ability is simply one of the wonderful mysteries of God. But if it gets twisted *that far* it can easily become false doctrine (like Jehovah's Witnesses believing that Michael the Archangel is Jesus Christ).

While the Bible clearly teaches that God can appear however He wishes, it's important for the Christian to remember that the Lord Jesus Christ is "the express image of his person" (Heb. 1:3). This means that JESUS CHRIST REPRESENTS GOD IN HIS TRUE PHYSICAL FORM. This additionally shows that when God created us "in his image", why we do not look like fire, clouds, doves or lambs, but MEN (Gen. 1:26-27). Theophanies and Christophanies provide evidence that, if God can appear as fire in a burning bush, and the Holy Ghost take on "a bodily shape like a dove", then Christ can appear as a star – "there shall come a STAR out of Jacob".

Twelve Reasons to Believe

We have now arrived at the end of our study. At this point, if you still subscribe to the Jupiter Theory as being the Star of Bethlehem (or any other theory), that's strictly between you and the Lord (or you and the Devil). Either way, you'll not hear a peep from me. But I believe the evidence presented in this book answers the mystery of Bethlehem's Star more completely. It ties words of scripture with other words of scripture, and doesn't end at a dead end when words like "Jupiter" are involved. Below is a list of 12 reasons why I believe that the Star of Bethlehem was a veiled appearance of the Lord Jesus Christ under the guise of the angel of the Lord.

REASON #1 - If the Star of Bethlehem was a veiled appearance of the Lord Jesus Christ under the guise of the angel of the Lord, it easily explains why the star was able to grab men's attention and hold that attention for over a year. It wasn't moving planets which were barely visible to the naked eye, and only noticeable through the study of star charts and measurements.

REASON #2 - If the Star of Bethlehem was a veiled appearance of the Lord Jesus Christ under the guise of the angel of the Lord, it easily explains why the star is no longer visible. The Star, unlike comets and conjunctioning planets, was a sign for Israel regarding the birth of Christ, and thus a one-time phenomenon (like the virgin birth).

REASON #3 - If the Star of Bethlehem was a veiled appearance of the Lord Jesus Christ under the guise of the angel of the Lord, it easily explains why no celestial, space-based phenomena has been able to conform with the details of scripture 100%, and why science and astronomy continue to guess at what the star "may have been", or either reject the concept outright.

REASON #4 - If the Star of Bethlehem was a veiled appearance of the Lord Jesus Christ under the guise of the angel of the Lord, it easily explains how the star was able to move and stop. Moving and stopping is self-explanatory when one realizes the "Star" was the angel of the Lord – it was ALIVE.

REASON #5 - If the Star of Bethlehem was a veiled appearance of the Lord Jesus Christ under the guise of the angel of the Lord, it easily explains how the star was able to make a southward turn at Jerusalem after first having traveled for hundreds of miles "from the east".

REASON #6 - If the Star of Bethlehem was a veiled appearance of the Lord Jesus Christ under the guise

IMAGE/public domain   The wise men following "his star"

Much scriptural evidence helps demonstrate that the Star of Bethlehem was probably not a real star, but an appearance of the angel of the Lord.

of the angel of the Lord, it easily explains how the star seemed to behave with intelligence, and was able to pinpoint the exact house of Joseph, Mary and the Babe. No celestial star is capable of such a feat. Especially since such stars would always have to be at or near the horizon in order to "lead", and then abruptly shift overhead once arriving at the destination. For a celestial star or planet, this shift would had to have taken place between Jerusalem and Bethlehem, a distance of only 5.5 miles. Imagine a REAL STAR moving from the horizon to overhead in only a 5 to 6 mile distance. It can't be done. Unless, of course, the "star" is much, much closer to the surface of the earth, and in that case, wouldn't have been stars or planets at all. It would have been something different. And upon arriving in Bethlehem, how would a celestial star single-out a house? Since stars are said to be "light years" away (the nearest star is reportedly a distance of 23.52 x 10^{12} miles away), how would you know which house you're being directed to? Celestial stars and space-based planetary phenomena fall way, way short in explaining this. But supernatural stars do not. Today's most popular Christian theory on the subject, one which supports the planet Jupiter as being the star, admits this when it states; "Objects at astronomical distances cannot literally point at or selectively illuminate a specific house."[17] But they worm their way out of this biblical fact by saying that "...the idea that the star pointed the magi to a specific house is not in the bible. It is an idea which has been added to the Biblical narrative."[18] A blatant lie!

REASON #7 - If the Star of Bethlehem was a veiled appearance of the Lord Jesus Christ under the guise

---

[17] Larson, Frederick A. "The FAQ: Frequently Asked Questions." . Frederick A. Larson, 2014. Web. May 2014. <www.bethlehemstar.net/about/faq/>.

[18] ibid.

of the angel of the Lord, it easily explains how the star was able to radiate light even though it was not a real planetary star. There are plenty of scriptural references showing angels radiating light, and this goes without saying that God Himself is said to be "Light" and a "consuming fire".

REASON #8 - If the Star of Bethlehem was a veiled appearance of the Lord Jesus Christ under the guise of the angel of the Lord, it does not *force* the date of Christ's birth to coincide with astronomical events, but leaves the date open to conform with scripture.

REASON #9 - If the Star of Bethlehem was a veiled appearance of the Lord Jesus Christ under the guise of the angel of the Lord, it easily explains why the SAME ANGEL not only appeared to the shepherds on the night of Christ's birth, but also to the wise men.

REASON #10 - If the Star of Bethlehem was a veiled appearance of the Lord Jesus Christ under the guise of the angel of the Lord, it easily explains why the SAME ANGEL actively played a role in signs and wonders, and in dealing with Israel in the Old Testament. The planet Jupiter is woefully defunct in this department.

REASON #11 - If the Star of Bethlehem was a veiled appearance of the Lord Jesus Christ under the guise of the angel of the Lord, it easily explains why it was able to appear as a celestial, sky-based phenomena, just like the pillar of cloud and fire which lead the Israelites out of Egypt, even thought the Bible associates BOTH events with ANGELS, and not real stars, or other types of elements found in nature.

REASON #12 - If the Star of Bethlehem was a veiled appearance of the Lord Jesus Christ under the guise of the angel of the Lord, it easily explains why it was *this angel* which appeared on the night of Christ's birth – and has never appeared in the sky since – *the Star of Bethlehem was the Lord Jesus Christ Himself!*

If the planet Jupiter *is* the Star of Bethlehem, it's completely inconsistent with the Bible's use of the word (if you're even concerned with the Bible's use of the word). The scriptures tell us to *"Prove all things; hold fast that which is good."* (1Thess. 5:21) The way to "prove" a thing is by FIRST testing it with scripture – not science.

For the planet Jupiter the news is not good. There are *no references* (zero) to the planet being used of God to do anything – much less to lead anyone to anywhere. And the planet has absolutely NOTHING to do with Luke's account of the Christmas Story. Instead, of the Bible's three appearances of the word, we find Jupiter linked to a false god, and an "image" falling to earth connected with the goddess "Diana" (see Acts 14:12-23 & 19:35). The Bible links Jupiter with false gods, goddesses, graven images and things coming to earth from space. This is all in contrast to the alternate theory of the "Star" being the "angel of the Lord". In which case we find the Bible not only linking stars with angels, but having the ability to lead, turn, stand still (all under the guise of CHRIST and LIGHT) and to tie Matthew's account with Luke.

This is not written to "slam" those that hold to the Jupiter Theory. It is what it is. It's what you get when you "prove" Jupiter with scripture. You get NOTHING. Nothing but a NEGATIVE RESPONSE when seeking light regarding Jupiter as the Star of Bethlehem. So if you find yourself offended at the Bible's summary of the word, after having believed that God may have used it to represent Bethlehem's Star, don't get mad at this author. Take your anger up with the Author of the Bible. He wrote it – I didn't. The bottom line is, you're now faced with a choice: Do I stand with THE BIBLE on stars and Jupiter, or do I stand with SCIENCE on stars and Jupiter?

The Certainty of the Words

In his 1979 book *The Star of Bethlehem*, British astronomer, David W. Hughes writes:

> "...the star was therefore most probably the sequence
> of Jupiter-Saturn events in 7 B.C. ... Of course we

cannot say that a miracle did not happen, only that it was not needed..."[19]

This is a typical explanation that many today give for the Star of Bethlehem. At least in this case, the astronomer makes the rare admission that "we cannot say that a miracle did not happen". Amen! And one especially cannot make the claim when only astronomical events are studied *to the exclusion of scripture*. Simply citing the Bible's account of the Star of Bethlehem found in Matthew 2:1-11 is not "Bible study" – it's Bible reading. And while it's commendable that when the Bible mentions "star", that one would BELIEVE THE WORDS, and then LOOK TO THE STARS to explain those words, Christians must realize that if one looks OUTSIDE THE BIBLE for answers, *before* looking INSIDE THE BIBLE for answers, a potential for error is created. This, I'm afraid, is what has happened to many well-meaning Christians in regards to the Star of Bethlehem. They read Matthew's account of the Star, believe it's a CELESTIAL PLANETARY STAR, and then end their study there. They forget to search out the subject by comparing scripture with scripture. This truncates the answer, and only gives them a half truth. And a half truth is never the whole truth.

The wise men *did* witness a literal event in the heavens. An event which, in many ways, looked much like the natural

[19] Hughes, David W. The Star of Bethlehem: An Astronomer's Confirmation. New York: Walker & Co, 1979. p. 198

appearance of a planetary star. But it was not Jupiter, Saturn or any celestial body. It was a special kind of "Angel" under a star-like appearance of Light. A miraculous sign and wonder, consistent with God's actions and methods of the past, which will never be able to be "proved" or "disproved" by astronomy or any other field of science. God's not worried half as much about "science" as He is about His WRITTEN WORDS. Yes, the "heavens declare the glory of God" (Psa. 19:1), but the details are found in the Bible.

> *"[20] Have not I WRITTEN TO THEE excellent things in counsels and knowledge, [21] That I might make thee KNOW THE CERTAINTY OF THE WORDS of truth; that thou mightest answer the words of truth to them that send unto thee?"*   Proverbs 22:20-21

The "certainty" of God's words are not found in science. They're found in the "excellent things in counsels and knowledge" which He has WRITTEN (read the verse again). So, if one want's to know more about the Star which appeared on Christmas night, DON'T GO LOOKING INTO ASTRONOMY to find verification of it's reality – look FIRST in the things which God has written. When this is done, you'll know "the certainty of the words of truth".

Legacy of the Wise Men

If the Star of Bethlehem was a sign to the Jews, why did men "from the east" follow the star and not men of Israel?

Isn't this a contradiction? No. Signs and wonders *are* for Israel, but the Jews are not always the only ones to respond to the phenomena.

If you'll recall, the original signs and wonders which the Lord worked upon Egypt, when Israel finally fled their captors, they were not only composed of the sons of Abraham, Isaac and Jacob, but a "mixed multitude" (Ex. 12:38). Meaning, SOME of the people which left Egypt, people which had also witnessed God's signs and wonders, were NOT ISRAELITES.

Likewise, if you study the earthly ministry of the Lord Jesus Christ, you will find that, by and large, it was the GENTILES WHICH FIRST RESPONDED to Christ's message – not the Jews. When the Lord Jesus first sent out his 12 apostles (all Jewish men), he sent them "not into the way of the Gentiles", but "to the lost sheep of the house of Israel." (Matt. 10:5-6). And yet, it was the Jewish people as a whole, unto whom Christ was first sent, which were instrumental in his death, stating; "His blood be on us, and on our children." (Matt. 27:25). Just before Stephen was martyred he testified:

"Ye stiffnecked and uncircumcised in heart and ears, ye do always resist the Holy Ghost: as your fathers did, so do ye. Which of the prophets have not your fathers persecuted? and they have slain them which shewed before of the coming of the Just One; OF WHOM YE HAVE BEEN NOW THE BETRAYERS AND MURDERERS." Acts 7:51-52

And Peter said:

"[22] Ye MEN OF ISRAEL, hear these words; Jesus of Nazareth, a man APPROVED OF GOD AMONG YOU BY MIRACLES AND WONDERS AND SIGNS, which God did by him in the midst of you, as ye yourselves also know: [23] Him, being delivered by the determinate counsel and foreknowledge of God, YE HAVE TAKEN, and by wicked hands have CRUCIFIED AND SLAIN: ... [36] Therefore LET ALL THE HOUSE OF ISRAEL KNOW assuredly, that God hath made that same Jesus, WHOM YE HAVE CRUCIFIED, both Lord and Christ." Acts 2:22-23&36

Even though Caesar, Pilate and Herod were involved, the apostles never directly accuse the Gentiles. Even after the crucifixion, it was the Jews which repudiated the Gospel. The majority of those which heard the word, and responded, both before and after Christ's death and resurrection, were Gentiles. Because of this Paul said:

"Then Paul and Barnabas waxed bold, and said, It was necessary that the word of God should FIRST HAVE BEEN SPOKEN TO YOU: but seeing YE PUT IT FROM YOU, and judge yourselves unworthy of everlasting life, lo, WE TURN TO THE GENTILES."

Acts 13:46

As a matter of fact, it was the Gentiles who were ascribed as having "great faith", not the Jews. Here are two outstanding examples:

"[22] And, behold, A WOMAN OF CANAAN came out of the same coasts, and cried unto him, saying, Have mercy on me, O Lord, thou Son of David; my daughter is grievously vexed with a devil. [23] But he answered her not a word. And his disciples came and besought him, saying, Send her away; for she crieth after us. [24] But he answered and said, I AM NOT SENT BUT UNTO THE LOST SHEEP OF THE HOUSE OF ISRAEL. [25] Then came she and

IMAGE/public domain

Christ and the Canaanite Woman
Jean-Francois de Troy (1743)

WORSHIPPED HIM, saying, LORD, help me. [26] But he answered and said, It is not meet to take the children's bread [Jesus, Israel's promised Messiah], *and to cast it to DOGS* [Gentiles]. *[27] And she said, TRUTH, LORD: yet the dogs eat of the crumbs which fall from THEIR MASTERS' table. [28] Then Jesus answered and said unto her, O woman, GREAT IS THY FAITH: be it unto thee even as thou wilt. And her daughter was made whole from that very hour."*

Matthew 15:22-28

This incident between the Lord Jesus Christ and a gentile woman, is one of the greatest and most powerful accounts in all of scripture. Look at those words. Jesus calls this woman a "dog". And what does she do? Does she get mad, call Jesus a "racist bigot", and then stomp off in a huff? No. Look at the words. She says; "Truth, Lord"! Do you see that? That's humility. She recognized that the politically incorrect WORDS which come out of Christ's mouth are TRUTH. Even when those words are supposedly "offensive" words. She knew that Jesus was The Authority, and his words were True. She didn't have to think twice about it. So if this Voice calls you a "dog", the same Voice which spoke the universe into existence, then amen, bless God, you're a dog! Jesus called this GREAT FAITH.

"[5] And when Jesus was entered into Capernaum, there came unto him A CENTURION, beseeching him, [6] And saying, Lord, my servant lieth at home sick of the palsy, grievously tormented. [7] And Jesus saith unto him, I will come and heal him. [8] The centurion answered and said, Lord, I am not worthy that thou shouldest come under my roof: but

SPEAK THE WORD ONLY, and my servant shall be healed. [9] For I am a man under authority, having soldiers under me: and I say to this man, Go, and he goeth; and to another, Come, and he cometh; and to my servant, Do this, and he doeth it. [10] When Jesus heard it, he marvelled, and said to THEM THAT FOLLOWED, Verily I say unto you, I HAVE NOT FOUND SO GREAT FAITH, NO, NOT IN ISRAEL."
Matthew 8:5-10 (also see Lk. 7:1-9)

Here is another profound example of a Gentile having "great faith". He understood THE TRUE POWER AND AUTHORITY of Christ. He recognized that Jesus' WORDS ALONE have the power to make a thing happen. For he too, in a very similar, yet simpler manner, could SPEAK and his words immediately come to pass; "... I SAY to this man, Go, and he goeth; and to another, Come, and he cometh." (compare *"And God SAID...and it was so"* Gen. 1) See that? And yet, when Christ stopped the tempest on the sea of Galilee, his disciples said; "WHAT MANNER OF MAN IS THIS, that even the WINDS and the SEA OBEY HIM!" (Matt. 8:27) Unlike the Roman Centurion, they failed to recognize the true power and authority of Christ' words. Because of this, they were accused of having "little faith" (Matt. 8:26).

These are the only two examples in all of scripture which ascribe someone with "great faith", and neither are Jews. This information is not meant to be anti-Semitic or against

Israel (God forbid). It's simply a fact. Regardless however, *"God hath not cast away his people which he foreknew."* (Rom. 11:2)

Some today make a big deal regarding the idea that the wise men were "magi" (the Greek root word for "magician" or practitioners of the occult). This may very well be the case. But more importantly, the Bible never uses the term "magician" nor refer to them as such. They are simply called "wise men", and this is done for a reason. They are men which "fell down, and worshipped him" once the Saviour was found (Matt. 2:11). Amen! These are not the actions of occultists, but CONVERTS. And so it is, wise men today still seek and worship The King. When Jesus spoke of those who would hear his words, do you know what he likened them unto?

> *"Therefore whosoever heareth these sayings of mine, and doeth them, I will liken him unto a WISE MAN, which built his house upon a rock:"*
>
> Matthew 7:24

"...and that Rock was Christ." 1Corinthians 10:4

These men were truly "wise men", and not "wise men after the flesh". For once they had literally SEEN HIM, they HUMBLED THEMSELVES, WORSHIPPED HIM, and gave gifts. These eastern Gentiles (not Jews) are the *first men recorded by scripture* as having "worshipped" God manifest in the flesh. Did you get that? That's their legacy. And if that's not "wisdom", I don't know the meaning of the word.

IMAGE/Can Stock Photo Inc.   The kings worship the King of Kings

"And when they were come into the house, they saw the young child with Mary his mother, and FELL DOWN, and WORSHIPPED HIM: and when they had opened their treasures, they PRESENTED UNTO HIM GIFTS; gold, and frankincense, and myrrh."

Matthew 2:11

Note how the actions of the wise men, upon seeing the young Child, reflect the following scriptures:

"HUMBLE YOURSELVES IN THE SIGHT OF THE LORD, and he shall lift you up."   *James 4:10*

"The FEAR OF THE LORD is the beginning of WISDOM: and the knowledge of the holy is understanding."   *Proverbs 9:10*

"The FEAR OF THE LORD is the instruction of WISDOM; and before honour is HUMILITY."

Proverbs 15:33

"[26] For ye see your calling, brethren, how that not many WISE MEN after the flesh, not many mighty, not many noble, are called: [27] But God hath chosen the foolish things of the world to confound the wise; and God hath chosen the weak things of the world to confound the things which are mighty; [28] And base things of the world, and things which are despised, hath God chosen, yea, and things which are not, to bring to nought things that are: [29] That no flesh should glory in his presence. [30] But of him are ye in Christ Jesus, who of God is made unto us wisdom, and righteousness, and sanctification, and redemption: [31] That, according as it is written, He that glorieth, LET HIM GLORY IN THE LORD."

1 Corinthians 1:26-31

Are you a wise man or wise woman? If not, the Lord is calling to you now. Why not receive Him?

"[10] And the angel said unto them, Fear not: for, behold, I bring you good tidings of great joy, which shall be to all people. [11] For unto you is born this day in the city of David a Saviour, which is Christ the Lord."
Luke 2:10-11

"[16] For God so loved the world, that he gave his only begotten Son, that whosoever believeth in him should not perish, but have everlasting life. [17] For God sent not his Son into the world to condemn the world; but that the world through him might be saved. [18] He that believeth on him is not condemned: but he that believeth not is condemned already, because he hath not believed in the name of the only begotten Son of God."   John 3:16-18

"For whosoever shall call upon the name of the Lord shall be saved."   Romans 10:13

"He that hath the Son hath life; and he that hath not the Son of God hath not life."   1John 5:12

"Man of Sorrows!" what a name;
For the Son of God, who came;
Ruined sinners to reclaim.
Hallelujah! What a Saviour!

Bearing shame and scoffing rude;
In my place condemned He stood;
Sealed my pardon with His blood.
Hallelujah! What a Saviour!

Guilty, vile, and helpless we;
Spotless Lamb of God was He;

"Full atonement!" can it be?
Hallelujah! What a Saviour!

Lifted up was He to die;
"It is finished!" was His cry;
Now in Heav'n exalted high.
Hallelujah! What a Saviour!

When He comes, our glorious King;
All His ransomed home to bring;
Then anew His song we'll sing:
Hallelujah! What a Saviour!

– Hallelujah! What a Saviour! by Philip P. Bliss, 1875

"...Where is he that is born KING of the Jews? for we have seen HIS STAR in the east, and are come to worship him." Matthew 2:2

"...I am the root and the offspring of David, and the bright and morning STAR." Revelation 22:16

THE END

Would You Be So Kind...

"I read this book,
and it was..."

Your thoughts on this book (pro or con) are appreciated. Why not take a quick minute to write a short review on Amazon.com or wherever you feel lead? The stark reality is, regardless of a book's subject, it will not remain in print if no one knows it exists. And a book that goes out of print, cannot edify other like-minded Christians who are hungry for Bible truth. In this age of global information, online book reviews help Bible-based books get found in an increasingly godless world.

Thank You!

ABOUT
THE AUTHOR

Jeffrey W. Mardis has been a born-again Christian since April, 1979, a lifelong student of the Bible, and has been writing and researching on end-times, Christian discernment issues since 1995. He is founder of *Sword-In-Hand Publishing*; a member of the *Christian Small Publishers Association* (CSPA), and the *Coalition for Independent Authors* (CIA). *Sword-In-Hand Publishing* was founded to instill a deeper knowledge and love for the Lord Jesus Christ and appreciation for the Final Authority of the *King James Bible*. Jeff resides in Campbellsville, Kentucky and has served in the graphic design field since 1993. He is an award-winning and internationally recognized logo and trademark designer; and an Independent, King James Bible-Believing Baptist.

"He which testifieth these things saith,
Surely I come quickly. Amen.
Even so, come, Lord Jesus."
REVELATION 22:20

www.swordinhandpub.com • swordinhandpub@gmail.com

INDEX

A

Aaron's rod 18

Abaddon (angel) 89

Abraham 38, 39, 41, 82, 83, 105, 112, 114, 135, 136, 151

Accidents of nature 21, 23

Adam 35, 36, 40

Adversary, The 27
See also Devil, Dragon, Lucifer, Prince of the power of the air, Satan

Amazon.com (business) 14

Angel Magic (book) 100

Angel(s) 15, 37, 50, 67-69, 71-75, 77, 78, 81-91, 93-97, 99-103, 105-119, 121-126, 128, 131, 133, 134, 136, 138, 139, 142-144, 146-148, 150, 158
See also Morning stars, Sons of God, Star(s)

Angel and the Shepherds, The (painting) 67

Angel of God, The 108-110, 116, 124, 125, 131, 138

Angel of the Lord, The 67, 105-119, 121, 122, 125, 128, 131, 134, 138, 142-144, 146, 147

Angels of the seven churches 72
See also Angels(s), Star(s)

Animal behavior 26

Animal, God appearing as 139-141
See also Dove, Lamb

Antichrist 47, 101

Apollyon See Abaddon

Apostles 151-152

Archangel 118, 141
See also Michael

Arcturus 88, 89
See also Constellation(s)

Astronomy 14, 19, 61, 82, 143, 150

Atmosphere of earth 76
See also First Heaven

B

Babel 95

Beast 35

Bethlehem 13-15, 17-21, 27, 30,

ALSO AVAILABLE
from Sword-In-Hand Publishing

Aliens Angels & Outer Space: A Biblical Investigation into Life Beyond Earth

A primer and introductory examination of extraterrestrial life. Contains a detailed look at Bible cosmology and scriptures which address angelology, demonology, life in the heavens and more. Great for small Bible study groups!

ISBN-10: 0-9819056-0-9

ISBN-13: 978-0-9819056-0-0

180 page paperback • 38 illustrations

$14.95 + s&h

What Dwells Beyond: The Bible Believer's Handbook to Understanding Life in the Universe

A vastly expanded and renamed Second Edition. Contains a history of extraterrestrialism from Genesis to the present, an illustrated guide to life forms, angelology, demonology, giantology, technology, prophecy and much, much more.

ISBN-10: 0-9819056-1-7

ISBN-13: 978-0-9819056-1-7

520 page paperback • 175 illustrations

$21.95 + s&h

www.swordinhandpub.com

CHRISTIAN TESTIMONIES AFTER READING
Aliens, Angels & Outer Space

"...As you know, the number of books on the topic of 'aliens' is burgeoning. I've read most of them (or at least very many), and your book is one of the best. It is, I believe, for the Christian, the finest introductory volume on the topic. You bring together all the important issues and information in a clear yet substantial manner. Your constant appeal throughout to the Holy Bible marks your book as one of the very few reliable and biblically sound treatments. And your use of the KJV tells me that you are aware of the tremendous problem the Church faces with the issue of modern 'Bible' versions and the contemporary Bible publishing industry..."

Pastor M. L.
Good Shepherd Lutheran Church (Independent)
November 23, 2010

─────────────────────────

"The Information found in this volume is amazing. It is an excellent aid to Bible study for the serious student of the word of God. It makes you THINK, and research for yourself. I recommend it to anyone who is seriously seeking truth in a world that is all about deceit."

Anonymous Reader
December 28, 2013

www.swordinhandpub.com

CPSIA information can be obtained at www.ICGtesting.com
Printed in the USA
LVOW07s0009140116

470557LV00026B/657/P